Marriage & Relationships

Preparation & Preservation

Keys to Enduring Happiness

by

David Sax, Jim Appleby & Vincent Murphy

Marriage & Relationships

by

David Sax, Jim Appleby and Vincent Murphy

First Printing – September, 1998

For more information, please contact:
Catholic Family Service Society
Marriage Preparation Program
449 Broad Street North
Regina, Saskatchewan
Canada S4R 2X8

Canadian Cataloguing in Publication Data

Sax, David J.

Marriage & relationships : preparation & preservation, keys to enduring happiness

Includes bibliographical references.
ISBN 1-894022-09-2

1. Marriage counselling. 2. Marriage – Religious aspects – Catholic Church.
I. Appleby, Jim, 1963- II. Murphy, Vincent, 1940-
III. Catholic Family Service Society (Regina, Sask.). IV. Title.

HQ10.S28 1998 259'.13 C98-920169-4

Cover Design by Mary Kay Vollhoffer, Regina, Saskatchewan

Designed, Printed and Produced in Canada by:
Centax Books, a Division of PrintWest Communications Ltd.
Publishing Director – Margo Embury
1150 Eighth Avenue, Regina, Saskatchewan, Canada S4R 1C9
Telephone (306) 525-2304 Fax: (306) 757-2439

TABLE OF CONTENTS

Acknowledgements

Each of us has several people who supported and helped us to bring this work to completion. We wish to especially acknowledge our marriage partners – Pam Appleby and Karen Sax, co-adventurers in living out Christian marriage.

We wish to acknowledge the many talents of Vincent Murphy in turning this body of knowledge into a user-friendly workbook filled with humour, life and hope.

Special acknowledgement is also given to Most Reverend James Weisgerber (now Bishop of the Catholic Diocese of Saskatoon) for his wisdom, direction and friendship during the seven years that Karen and David Sax volunteered with other couples in Regina to develop marriage preparation materials which became the basis for this workbook.

A special thank you to Reverend John Prince, Judicial Vicar of the Regina Regional Marriage Tribunal, for his advice in elucidating the canonical aspects of the material presented.

Our appreciation to Bishop Allan Grundahl of the Saskatchewan Synod of the Evangelical Lutheran Church for reviewing the work and offering suggestions to improve the text.

This workbook would not be available if not for the vision and financial support of the Catholic Family Service Society and the Catholic Family Service of Regina Foundation Inc. All sales of this workbook will go back into the Foundation to aid in the continued services to families in distress who seek counselling from the Society in Regina.

Jim Appleby and David Sax

Critical Reviews

I have read the manual on marriage preparation and I am most impressed. Clearly the whole book is well thought out by those who have a great deal of experience in this field. The section on Christian Marriage should be extremely useful in helping people come to a deeper understanding of the meaning and possibilities of married life based on Christian beliefs. Each topic provides the facilitator with a good tool to enable dialogue with both partners while it gives them the information needed to examine the spiritual side of their marriage. Your presentation of the sacramental character and dignity of marriage is a much-needed illumination of a topic that needs to be addressed in our present society.

Reverend J.R. Prince
Chancellor and Head of the Regional Marriage Tribunal
for the Archdiocese of Regina

Written in an easy reading style and clearly laid out with the immediate questions raised by people treated first . . . Why marry? . . . Why have a CHRISTIAN wedding? . . . What about divorce? . . . Why not live together first to prepare? . . . Good humour was injected periodically, and very appropriate. I am impressed with your work, and would be most happy to recommend it. I especially appreciate the personal spiritual emphasis. I particularly endorse your many references to the shortness of life and the need to attend to what is worth the attention in the days of marriage given to Christian partners.

Bishop Allan A. Grundahl
Saskatchewan Synod
Evangelical Lutheran Church in Canada

Marriage & Relationships

Catholic Family Service Society
Marriage Preparation Program

Why Do People Come to Marriage Preparation Courses?

There are many reasons. Perhaps you were encouraged to attend by your partner, priest, minister or counsellor. Perhaps you have identified a need to have a better understanding of your relationship with your partner. You may want to be better prepared for what lies ahead.

Whatever the reason or reasons, **you** are the one who made the final decision to attend. It is you who will learn from the readings, discussions and exercises offered in this workbook.

Congratulations on your decision to learn and grow in your relationship!

To paraphrase the message of St. Francis of Assisi, whatever you need in your relationship with another person – give it away. What you give away with love and respect will be returned to you in abundance.

There is an old saying, "When a woman marries a man, she hopes he will change. When a man marries a woman he hopes she won't. They're both disappointed."

Dr. Melvyn Kinder

Welcome To Marriage & Relationships

These keys to the preparation and preservation of marriage relationships are intended to allow as much flexibility as possible.

The entire workbook or only a few selected exercises could be used by couples on a one-to-one basis or by facilitators in conjunction with other marriage preparation programs.

Priests, parish workers, host couples or others could use the workbook as a single teaching tool.

Couples could also be provided with workbooks and be asked to do their reading and exercises at home. Discussion around a particular topic could then be held with the marriage preparation facilitator or counsellor.

The nature of modern-day relationships requires flexibility in the presentation of marriage preparation programs. This workbook is designed to allow individual couples, churches, parishes and family service agencies that flexibility.

Sample Itinerary to assist in the use of this workbook:

Week One – Introductory Session and Christian Marriage
Readings and exercises: Christian Marriage

Week Two – Discussion around Introductory Session and Christian Marriage
Readings and exercises: Marriage & Family

Week Three – Discussion of Marriage & Family
Readings and exercises: Conflict Resolution and Communication

Week Four – Discussion around Conflict Resolution and Communication
Readings and exercises: Sexual Intimacy

Week Five – Readings and discussion around Cycles of Marital Growth
Readings and exercises: Conclusion

NOTE: Marriage preparation facilitators may wish to use tools such as the pre-marriage inventory of a Myers-Briggs Personality Inventory as complementary learning for their couples.

Setting Sail On The Seas Of Marriage

Life is a journey. Learning and growing from within is a journey. As in all journeys, we will meet our good days and not so good days.

That's life!

Imagine that this time in your relationship is the beginning of a sea voyage. You are both co-captains of the Good Sailing Ship "Love". (Sorry, the Love Boat idea has been taken.)

In order for you to have a worthwhile and generally pleasant journey you must both agree on a destination. You cannot be squabbling over direction and speed nor fighting over whether the sails should be up or down.

The journey will have its share of "fair wind" days when your little boat will be carried over the gently rolling seas of life.

It's easy to sail through the seas of life together on these sunny days and starlit nights.

Then there will be rainy, drizzly days when you are "becalmed". "Dead in the water" is another term. You will need patience, a willingness to listen, to acknowledge the other person's needs.

"If there is no wind, row."

Latin Proverb

Just to balance it off, and to make it more challenging, there will also be days of wild and furious sea winds, great roaring waves and plenty of "green water" across your bow. Every bit of love, team work, combined effort and compassion will be needed to help you both "ride out the storm".

"Calm seas do not a sailor make."

Newfoundland saying

You have very little, if any, control of when and perhaps if you will ever reach your original goal within the time or objective limits you have set.

Life is made up of both beautiful and stormy days. There will be enough storms coming your way without creating more of your own.

"We cannot control the winds but we can adjust the sails."

Anonymous

Introductory Session

So, You Want To Get Married

Why? There are many personal answers to this question. There are fundamental keys to success. In this session we'll explore the foundations of loving relationships that eventually lead to the decision to get married.

There was a time when marriage was regarded as the "only way to go". Couples were either married or lived in sin. That was it!

Then along came the 1960s and 70s when a wave of doom sayers predicted that the institution of marriage was on the way out.

Free Love and casual relationships were said to be the way of the future.

What happened? Not much. Marriage is still the most central and crucial relationship for the majority of Canadians. Nine out of ten individuals born within Canada will eventually marry at least once. Marriage, then, is still the most popular voluntary institution within our society.

Marriage & Divorce

It seems, however, that we cannot mention marriage without mentioning divorce. It is a sad truth that some four out of ten first marriages end in divorce. There is often less time between "I Do" and "Adieu". Why? Like marriage, there are many personal answers to this question. There is, again, one fundamental key to success in marriage.

Events leading up to divorce, the divorce and the subsequent fallout cause tremendous upset in the lives of family and friends. Everyone in the circle is affected. Children often become the unknowing or unwilling or even unrecognized victims of separation and divorce.

The real human cost of divorce is enormous in terms of emotional hurt, grief, anger, loneliness, desperation and a sense of failure for all concerned.

The forty percent failure rate in marriages would indicate that, more than ever, it is essential for couples to build a firm foundation for their marriage. Research consistently demonstrates that couples who do not resolve problems and misunderstandings during their engagement will carry those issues into their marriage.

When Did You Begin?

Here's an interesting question. When did you begin preparing for marriage? Sure, this may be your first formal marriage preparation course but you actually began preparing for marriage through the lifelong experience of living with your family. How did your mother and father get along? What did you learn about marriage from relatives and friends?

Your marriage preparation continued through your school years and previous romantic relationships. You learned from both your positive and negative experiences and from those of your friends. Movies, songs, books and television shows all added to your understanding and opinions. You have already established an attitude about how marriage should work as a result of these combined experiences.

What is the Purpose of this Course?

Communication and **conflict resolution** skills are effective keys in helping couples through the first and subsequent years of marriage. Research has shown that couples who took a marriage preparation course which presented these skills enjoyed increased abilities in resolving conflicts in their relationships. They were also more likely to search for professional help as they worked together as loving, supportive and committed partners in marriage.

Here are the places we will visit on our journey into marriage preparation:

- ***So, You Want To Get Married***
- ***Why Get Married Within A Christian Church?***
- ***Your Past Is Connected To Your Present Marriage Plans***
- ***Different Styles Of Living Can Create Conflict***
- ***Good Communication***
- ***Sexuality Is Our Humanness***
- ***Growth Means Change***
- ***Blended Family: Mine, Yours & Ours***
- ***Whose Money Is It?***
- ***Humour Helps***

What is the Key to Success in Marriage?

"Mutual commitment amongst all parties is the key to success in any relationship, project or journey."

So Why Get Married Anyway?

The media continually tells us about the demise of marriage. There is a barrage of statistics and personal histories referring to the unhappiness of married people. "Look! See how many marriages have failed!" exclaim the media.

All this counter-marriage information begs the questions. Why would anyone consider having a Christian marriage? Why not just go with the flow and live in a common-law relationship?

"After all, isn't living common-law a great way to prepare for marriage? We'll just live together for a while and find out if we are compatible. That way we can prevent any problems before getting married."

If the above statement were true, why is it that people living common-law, who then become married, fare no better – or sometimes worse – than those who commit to a Christian (legal) marriage?

It becomes obvious that a common-law relationship is not necessarily a valid marriage preparation program.

Most couples seeking to get married, that have been living together, believe they are not married. There are, however, legal responsibilities in a common-law relationship.

Let's look at some of the aspects of common-law relationships versus a Christian (legal) marriage.

Legal Ramifications of Common-law Relationships and Marriage

The following may come as a surprise to many common-law couples. A common-law relationship, from a point of law, is no longer the cordial, informal situation it was in the past. Provincial legislatures, within the Government of Canada, and various federal laws, within the United States, have recognized the common-law relationship as **legally binding**.

Depending on the amount of time the couple has spent within the live-in relationship, various legal responsibilities are similar to those of legally married couples.

Debts and assets accrued during the common-law relationship could be legally assigned to either of the individuals in the relationship. Co-signed loans for cars, mortgages, and items such as furniture and appliances purchased for the household are some examples of accrued debts and assets. All are subject to rules and regulations that vary in different parts of Canada and the U.S.

Couples who are now living in (or are considering) a common-law relationship or are planning to become married within the Christian Church are encouraged to make themselves familiar with the legal duties and responsibilities within their present and future relationship.

This information is available through legal aid societies, public legal education forums and individual law offices.

"Just Being Together" – Are These the Ties that Bind?

"Research has shown that living together is not an automatic overture to happy marriage. Several recent studies have demonstrated that the divorce rate is higher among couples who live together before marriage than among those who do not.

"This is a troublesome finding, because a strong argument for cohabitation has been that it would slow the divorce rate. Presumably, living together would allow a couple to make a more informed decision about marriage.

"Now, in our culture of divorce, the fears have undergone a curious reversal. Except for the worry about AIDS (and other sexually transmitted diseases), premarital sex and living together are considered safe. But marriage is considered dangerous. After all, marriage fails half the time and brings misery to those who venture into it. The logic is, if you don't marry, you won't divorce.

"The argument that cohabitation enables people to iron out flaws in the relationship or that it promotes more stable marriages has not been proven correct; living together is not a preventive for divorce."

(*The Good Marriage*, by Judith Wallerstein and Sandra Blakeslee, Warner Books Inc. 1271 Avenue of the Americas, N.Y., N.Y. 10020, 1995)

Living together as a selection process is not like maintaining a wardrobe. "I'm tired of this sweater. It doesn't fit like it did when I bought it. Oh well, I'll just get rid of it and try on something else!"

The lure of common-law living is that it seems to be a relationship with no strings attached. "Let's try this one on for size!" The idea being that you can enter or leave with ease. This is not so. There are many unacknowledged emotional and financial strings that can bind very tightly.

A common-law relationship tends not to demand equal responsibility from each partner. It can become a tragic breeding ground for unrealistic rescue fantasies and dependency. Living together at first is easy – no big commitments – no promises – no problem.

The ending, however, will not be as easy as casting off a garment. Many bonds have been formed, no matter how informal the relationship. The breakup of extended cohabitation can be just as gut wrenching and destructive as a divorce.

Things are Going to be Different the Day After Marriage!

Many couples who have been dating each other or living together for years eventually decide to get married. They falsely assume that life will go on as before. It is important to realize that the level of commitment increases dramatically after marriage.

The ship never leaves the dock in a common-law relationship. There is always the opportunity for either person to "jump ship" should things not be going along well between the partners. You cannot jump ship as easily while sailing the open seas of marriage.

Again, it is mutual commitment that will make the relationship work.

Working at Having a Good Marriage

Fifty couples who reported positive marriage relationships were interviewed for the book *The Good Marriage* (Wallerstein and Blakeslee, Warner Books, 1995). On the basis of their study they proposed nine psychological tasks that challenged men and women throughout their life together.

Here is a review of the tasks:

1. Both members in a marriage need to detach themselves emotionally from their families of childhood. Their need is to commit their emotional attachment **to each other** in their marriage relationship.

2. There is a need to build intimacy and togetherness, to expand the sense of "self" to include the other person. At the same time there is a need to carve out a place of independence for each person. A healthy marriage relationship is based on "us/us/us!" rather than "me/me/me!" It's a balance of sharing a life together while still maintaining individual autonomy. It is true equality.

3. Expand the circle to include children. This requires a balance between the needs of the children and the need to continue to nurture the marriage relationship.

4. Meet and deal with the inevitable trials, tribulations and crisis situations. Marriage is life. It is not perfect. Illness, accidents, injuries, death, job loss and natural disasters go on – married or not. The couple recognizes their commitment to each other. They learn to manage the stress. The marriage will not fade but will reinvent itself and take on new forms as they grow in their learning.

5. Find ways to resolve differences without exploiting each other, being violent or giving away one's heart's desires.

6. Establish and maintain a pleasurable sex life.

7. Share healthy humour and laughter. Work at keeping the marriage interesting. A good marriage is a mixture of everything life has to offer. It can be playful, serious, sometimes flirtatious, sometimes difficult and cranky – but always full of life!

8. Provide the emotional nurturing and encouragement that everyone needs – kind words, thoughtful deeds.

9. Remember the joy of your courtship. Sustain the innermost core of your marriage by drawing on the sustenance and renewal of the images and fantasies of your first days together. Work to maintain that joyful glow over a lifetime together.

(Original source: Wallerstein and Blakeslee, 1995: pages 313-314)

Christian Marriage

WHY GET MARRIED WITHIN A CHRISTIAN CHURCH?

The decision to enter a Christian marriage can be made for various reasons. Being in a Christian marriage can also have different meanings for each partner. The attitude of a particular church towards Christian marriage and your reasons for being married within that church can vary as well.

Similarly, your parent's view of marriage in relation to the church may differ from yours.

If you have been living in a common-law relationship,
now is a good time to ask yourself
"Why, after this period of time, do I wish to be formally married?"

"For Better or for Worse"

Traditional Christian marriages within mainline churches utilize the phrase "for better or for worse" in the wedding vows.

It is crucial at this time of commitment to ask what this phrase really means to you personally and as a couple.

The journey of life in marriage is marked with many peaks and valleys. Personality differences and flaws, debilitating illness or injury, job loss and the pressures of parenting are just a few things that can test the strength of a couple's commitment. These factors and just the ordinary business of day-to-day life lay out a journey of life that is not always pleasant. Life together comes with no guarantees that "everything will always be just fine".

It is crucial to clarify what the commitment of marriage and its permanence means to each partner in the relationship.

Christian Marriage

Marriage is a Sacrament*

The commitment of marriage is sacred in every Christian Church, and is a sacrament in the Catholic Church and some others – the moment of Christ's presence and permanence in our lives. An openly Christian marriage thus truly represents God's unifying love through Jesus Christ.

The sacrament of the marriage ceremony is more than a fancy civil ceremony with its boisterous celebrations. It marks the source of grace to live our Christianity in this new relationship with one another and with Christ as a partner. It is a new vocation – a commitment to our unconditional love for life – and salvation.

The Christian marriage is witness to God's love for us as individuals and as a couple. Our commitment to this marriage is a sign to the world that we acknowledge God's love through Christ.

Every valid marriage between two baptized persons is sacred in all Christian denominations and is a sacrament in the Catholic tradition. It is a marriage bond, lifelong and exclusive. The marriage bond requires each partner to be faithful to the other, to share the other's life and to give freely of spiritual and material support.

Christian Intentionality

The Christian marriage reflects what St. Paul calls a "high mystery", having to do with Christ and His Church.

As Christians in marriage, our minds and hearts are open to live in the context of the Christian message. We believe in a reality beyond the here and now. We are challenged to serve each other in the commitment of our marriage – sometimes in unselfish, mysterious or even sacrificial ways.

Whatever happens as a couple, we are going to mingle our two lives completely into one, forever. To live, love and grow together. To raise children and build a family. To love God and humanity from this centre of family love.

* The Catholic tradition holds marriage as a sacrament – the presence of Christ – while other Christian traditions consider it to be holy and solemn – a sacred witness to the love of Christ. Where it is more appropriate for your tradition to use sacred in the following text, please do so.

MELDING AND MOULDING

The Christian marriage calls upon the partners to touch and shape the unique personal qualities of each other. We assume responsibility for the growth and destiny of our spouse. Each partner is the contact point for God's providential love and Christ's eternal plan of redemption. We are the ministers and bearers of the sacrament to each other.

In the sacrament, the conjugal love of the couple is mingled with and supercharged by the love of Christ. The high mystery is revealed in Christ. He is the light, the key to meaning and reality. The key that unlocks the relationship to grow beyond our fears. Through Christ we become ourselves. We become fully human.

IS LASTING MARRIAGE POSSIBLE?

Tony and Marian, who have been married for over ten years, went to a party. The conversation at the party turned to marriage and divorce. They soon discovered that of the ten couples at the party only four were in their original marriage.

Modern society puts a lot of pressure on our traditional beliefs and institutions. The question is often asked, "Is lifelong marriage possible in our culture?" Good question!

The past forty years have been hard on the institution of marriage. There is a sense of pessimism about the viability of marriage as more people opt for less formal relationships. Young people and separated persons often turn to informal arrangements as their way to commit to each other. This may be seen as an attempt to avoid being disappointed about a marriage "not working out".

These informal relationships do have some connection to the social and emotional relevance of a marriage. This informality, however, leaves a situation where nothing is avoided and possibly nothing is resolved.

Despite the widely publicized trend toward informal relationships, lifelong satisfying marriage is just as common, throughout the world, as divorce.

Passion is Not Enough

"Love is the only answer!" "Love will see us through!"

While these sayings are all very nice, they do not deal with what really makes a relationship work in the long run. Passion, idealism and determination are not enough. They may be the starter for the fire but a good supply of wood is needed to keep the embers burning. You may have had an experience similar to Tony and Marian. How many "true love" or "marriages made in heaven" relationships amongst your family and friends have faltered and ended in disappointment and divorce?

"If love is the answer, could you rephrase the question?"
Lily Tomlin

Faith in Christ's Love for Us Makes the Difference

If passion, idealism and determination are not enough, what does it take? Social scientists have long recognized that a marriage lasts when two people allow themselves to change and grow. Yet they are still able to maintain their love and commitment toward each other. This is a natural force in nature.

Change requires growth. Growth requires change. Love in this case is more than a feeling. It is a personal choice and a continuing behaviour that will help sustain the marriage.

There is more to this than human love, adapting to change or motivation for growth. The added dimension is an active, living faith in God's love. This can be the greatest resource for a lasting marriage.

A Christian marriage is more than a marriage between two individuals. It is a marriage between three – wife, husband and Jesus Christ. The love, compassion and healing power of Jesus Christ are there as we struggle, suffer, become confused or disillusioned. We can rely upon Jesus to "be there for us" as a third partner. A partner who provides the strength for us to go on – together.

People who attend religious services every week not only have more enduring marriages than people who shun organized religion, but they are happier and healthier, a report (from Statistics Canada) released yesterday say.

Source: *THE GLOBE & MAIL, September 16, 1998*

Saying "I Do . . . "

We are changed forever by our "I do . . . ".

Imagine that you have two glasses of clear water. Your name is on one glass and your spouse's name is on the other.

Now imagine adding some food colouring to each glass. One blue, the other yellow.

Take a glass pitcher and label it "I do." Pour the blue and yellow water into the pitcher. What happens? The two colours are blended.

Now pour equal amounts of the blended water back into the glasses.

Think about it. Once you enter into a relationship with another person, they will always be part of you. You can never go back to your original self.

God's Love Makes Things Possible

St. John in his first letter says: "We love because God loved us first" (1 John 4: 19). Our love for God is possible because He loves us first. St.John also points out that our love for one another is only made real and perfect by living in the faith of God's love for us. St. John says: "This is what love is; it is not that we have loved God, but that He loved us and sent us His Son" (1 John 4: 10).

St. John proposes that God's love can make the difference in how we love and how we live. St. Paul also believed this as stated in the letter to the Philippians: "I am no longer trying for perfection by my own efforts, the perfection that comes from the law, but I want only the perfection that comes through the faith in Christ, and is from God and based on faith" (Philippians 3: 9).

God's love makes the difference in a Christian marriage. It's the individual's acknowledgement of the love and compassion of Christ in his or her life. This love really helps us determine how we will love our partner and how we will live together.

"With This Ring . . . "

The wedding ring reflects unity – the continuing love given to us when Christ is acknowledged as a true partner in the marriage. The ring is a symbol of a completeness with no specific beginning or end. The ring represents the circle – the most ancient symbol for life, love and eternity.

The unity of love is only possible because God loves us first. God gives us the completeness of love through Jesus. The beginning and the end of love is ours when Jesus is a partner in our marriage.

What is perfect? Nothing in humankind's creation comes very close to perfection. We constantly see examples of social disorder and mechanical failure in our lives. Even our attempts at loving are far from perfect. God's love, however, is perfect. It is unconditional, comforting and healing.

The wonderful thing about Christian marriage, then, is that you can give up the struggle to reach the impossibility of perfection in your marriage. God's love is for the imperfect in all of us. Loving each other in spite of our imperfections brings hope and freedom in our lives.

People Confuse a Christian Marriage with Being Married in a Church

Simply "booking the church" for the wedding does not reflect the deep spiritual meaning of a Christian marriage. Faith is a gift from God. A Christian marriage is a gift from God as well. These are gifts offered to you from Christ. Your wedding vows include acknowledging Christ as your third partner. This is your opportunity to ask for the gift of faith and the gift of Christian marriage.

God doesn't ask a lot of questions. God accepts you where you are in your faith right now. Walk with God – with Jesus as your third partner. It is up to you to ask the questions. In Luke 11:9-10, Jesus says: "Ask and you will receive; seek and you will find; knock and the door will be opened to you. For everyone who asks will receive; and he who seeks will find and the door will be opened to anyone who knocks."

Your wedding is a celebration of your love and unity. It is the opportunity to welcome Jesus as your third partner. Ask Him for the gifts of faith and a Christian marriage. The Christian marriage is yours to have because you choose each other and Christ in front of an assembly of believers. The gowns, guests, music, presider and ceremony are just that – ceremony.

> ***The Christian marriage is the presence of Christ in and between the two of you witnessed before your community of people. Thus, your marriage is truly a circle of love and unity.***

A Christian Marriage has Some Basic Prerequisites

We have learned how a Christian marriage differs from a secular marriage. Thus, there are certain prerequisites to ensure that both parties understand and acknowledge the gifts of love and commitment to each other and Christ.

Here are the requirements of a Christian marriage:

- Both people come to accept and commit themselves to the other freely.
- Their free choice is made without social (family, friends) pressure, obligation, duress or coercion. This free choice is made as equals in each other's eyes.
- A personal faith in God's love for us manifest (as revealed) in the gift of Jesus as saviour to all.
- An openness to personal change and growth; an openness to the needs and gifts of one's spouse; an openness to sharing life with one another as equals.
- A whole-hearted, freely given commitment to each other. A mutual expectation that this commitment will be lived out for life. That this commitment will be shared with others as evidence of Christ's presence among us.

Christian Marriage – Exercise #1, see page 105.

Practice It or Lose It, Sharing the Gift of Christian Joy

A Christian marriage is a shared experience between three partners. It is important to realize that the practice of being a Christian must be sustained as partners or as a team. Otherwise, there is a danger of slipping into nonchalance in the expression of what makes your marriage a Christian marriage.

Here are some ways to ensure the joy and commitment of your Christian marriage:

1. Establish some regular personal and shared habits of faith.

- Praying as a couple can help you through both times of difficulty and celebration.
- The simple act of saying grace at mealtimes as a shared experience demonstrates your gratitude to God.
- Scripture study. Share and discuss a book of selected scripture verses.
- Instruction in one's faith through counselling or group meetings.
- Regular attendance at church celebrations and liturgies as an expression of your joyful Christian commitment.
- Help instruct others and your children in the faith of the community of believers.

2. An openness, a joy, a celebration of your belief and a willingness to be responsive to the needs of others in your community of believers, extended family and the family of humanity throughout the world.
3. Active, vocal and visible forgiveness of self, and for others.
4. Responding to and acting in Christ's call for us to love one another.

Love is a Decision

Remember the romantic love feeling? Passion Plus! Then the sexual love. A craving for satisfaction!

The love of Christ in a Christian marriage goes beyond passion and craving. It brings in the element of commitment which leads to responsible behaviour. St. Paul said it best in his famous words on love (One Corinthians 13: 4-9).

Love is always patient and kind;
It is never jealous;
It is never boastful or conceited;
It is never rude or selfish;
It does not take offense and is
not resentful.
Love has no pleasure in other people's
sins but delights in the truth;
It is always ready to excuse,
to trust, to hope
and to endure whatever comes.

Each of the word descriptions from St. Paul's writing are actual behaviours which we can practice. Let's examine this thoughtful writing more closely. But first a look at two keys words – always and never.

"Always" is eternal – a long time indeed. That's the commitment we make in a loving relationship. "Always" can also be expressed as "all ways". Patience and kindness as expressed in our emotional and physical actions – and reactions. In the things we say and do. Always and all ways, forever.

"Never" is also total commitment – and an impossibility. As humans we are subject to making mistakes, saying the wrong thing or just "blowing it". God has given us the ability to recognize human frailty in ourselves and others. We have the ability to forgive and move on to a new understanding. It is our choice!

Let's Examine St. Paul's Words More Closely

- **Love is Always Patient and Kind:** Patience and kindness come from the very centre of our attitude towards ourselves and others. Being patient and kind means being able to wait and deal with your own expectations later.

  You also allow your partner to achieve their own accomplishments and make their own mistakes. Your attitude allows them to be "themselves", and appreciate them for **who** they are. Your attitude of patience and kindness does not set up rules. You do not demand that they live up to who and what **you** think they should be.

- **Love is Never Jealous:** Jealousy is not limited to "being jealous" about attention or affection given to another person. You can be jealous about another's time, energy and interests. Jealousy is possessiveness and control. It is pre-occupation with the real possibility of rejection or even loss.

  Love has no room for such destructive forces. Possessiveness, control, fearfulness, selfishness and the resulting turmoil are not part of Christ's calling for respect for the other person's dignity. Christ's love requires the open expression of faith in each other's goodness.

- **Love is Never Boastful or Conceited:** Boastfulness is a self-infatuation (self-inflation). It's like someone pumping themselves up with a tank of compressed air. They declare themselves an authority on, well, just about everything. Being right is more important than being fair or equal. The communication style is based on criticism, belittling, teasing, provocation and misunderstanding.

  Christ's love brings only humility and acceptance of your own strengths and weaknesses. You take comfort in your own neediness and gifts to each other.

- **Love is Never Rude or Selfish:** Ow! That hurt! When we are hurt our first reaction is to take offence – to be insulted. We act out with blaming, mistrust and defensiveness. It causes us to withdraw from our spouse. There is isolation and rejection. Not a very healthy or healing environment.

  Now consider how the love of Christ can bring you to the spirit of openness, honesty and forgiveness for your spouse. This love seeks out unity rather than isolation.

- **Love Delights in the Truth:** Imagine having the choice of drinking from a pool of crystal pure water or a polluted pond. A relationship based on deception, manipulation and coercion is like a polluted pond. The love of Christ has no room for the "relationship pollutants" of wrongs and hurts.

  The crystal pure delight of truth is to enjoy one another's openness, honesty and the talents of each other. Celebrate the joy of your truths. Delight in and speak highly of one another's strengths, goodness and sincere efforts. Complaining and criticizing one another will only muddy the waters.

- **Love is Always Ready to Excuse:** Your love commitment includes being able to excuse (forgive) and not keep a running record of wrongs and hurts. Expect good things from one another. Accept and believe in your partner even when you do not understand his or her behaviour. The love of Christ affirms that we can be forgiven. We can forgive. We can mend and heal. We can try again.

- **Love is Always Ready to Trust, to Hope and to Endure:** Consider these comforting words in all things you say and do with each other. They are words of commitment and reflect how the love of Christ makes it possible to speak in a trustful and trusting manner. Use words and deeds that are hopeful in nature.

  We know that the commitment of Christ's love and our love will help us "hang in there" during times of difficulty and suffering. Hope allows us to wait for a new day. We trust in the good that Christ can bring out of every situation as we journey together.

"If you have love,
You will do all things well."
Thomas Merton

Christian Marriage – Exercise #2, see page 106, and also Exercise # 3, page 108.

Our Love Things to Do List

Mend a quarrel
Share some treasure
Give a soft answer
Encourage
Keep a promise
Find the time
Listen
Apologize if you were wrong
Be gentle
Laugh a little
Laugh a little more
Laugh a lot
Learn to grieve a loss
Express your gratitude
Welcome a stranger
Gladden the heart
Take pleasure in the beauty
and wonder of creation
Speak your love
Speak it again
Speak it still once again

Vincent Murphy

Marriage & Family

Your Past Is Connected To Your Present Marriage Plans

Let's take a journey in a Time Machine.

The next time you visit your parents, ask to spend some time looking through their photo albums. Take a look at those neat old photos of your grandparents, great-grandparents or even double or triple great-grandparents.

While you are cruising the pages, look for aunts, uncles, cousins, family and friends.

These are not just ancient faces staring from fading photographs.

They are a part of you and everything you think and do.

"Wow! Is this possible? Aren't I my own person? Don't I make decisions based on what **I** think and feel?"

Yes. And no.

Our life experiences and learning are intertwined with the lives of those who came before us. Your parents were influenced by their parents, family, friends and life/work experiences, and so on down the line. This is called conditioning.

Let's open the photo albums. Hey, there's a stern old face. So, Great-Grandfather was a – well – let's say he was hard to get along with. We could call him a tyrant, dictator or oppressor, but "hard to get along with" will do for now.

As you can expect, this man's actions and attitudes would have left a deep and lasting impression on his wife, children, family and friends. He may have set up fears, angers and limitations that were passed on through the generations. In some way you may still be affected by his actions and attitudes.

Now let's flip a few pages in the photo album. There she is! Your dear Auntie. Wasn't she a sweetheart? She was great to talk to and showed genuine interest in your growing up and going to school.

Her kindness affected you. You try to live your life through her example. She, like your grumpy great-grampa, will have some influence in how you react to and deal with the everyday business of living your life.

> ***We are influenced and thus conditioned by others from our very beginning. As children we learn to mimic the actions and attitudes of those around us.***

Our expectations can often be based on values demonstrated by others. Fears, anger, conflict, attitudes, prejudices, communication skills and willingness to change are only a few aspects of our lives that can be influenced by our past.

Families of origin are wide and varied in the Canadian culture. The traditional single culture family is rare indeed.

Let's go back over those old photos again. There, below the photo of your Mom's Uncle Mike with his Model A car. That's Mike and his wife, Maria. So, Mike was Irish and Maria was French-Cree Metis! There's a good example of both a cross-culture and inter-racial marriage.

It's a wonder that they got along, what with their many differences. They must have really loved each other. Something else came into play, no doubt. They must have worked hard to understand and appreciate their differences **as well as** the things they had in common.

Looking back at those old photos makes us aware that, in many ways, we are influenced to some degree by our family of origin. Our expectations, of course, will vary from those of our partner who has a completely different history of family life experiences.

We can make the best of our past experiences and the influence others had on us. We can learn to change and compromise. We can make the decision to live and learn as a team. As with any team, commitment, communication and effective problem solving are the keys to a successful relationship.

Is it possible to "recondition" ourselves in much the same way that a modern photo lab could put a smile on dear old great-grampa's face?

Here's a story to illustrate how we can be influenced by the past.

> ***Jonathan watched as Elaine prepared a ham for supper. He noticed that Elaine always cut a two-inch thick piece off the end before placing the ham in the roasting pan.***
>
> ***"Why do you cut that piece off the end?" he asked.***
>
> ***Elaine replied that's what her mother always did and she was just continuing the practice. Later Elaine phoned her mother to ask about this little cooking quirk. Mother said that her mother did the same thing and she just continued the practice. When Elaine phoned her grandmother for an explanation, she was told:***
>
> ***"I always cut a piece off the end of the ham because it was too big for my little roasting pan!"***

Family Backgrounds, Values and Expectations – Exercise #1, see page 117.

Getting Along with Yourself and Other People – It's Different for Everyone

Remember Grade School? How can we forget? You must do this and you can't do that. Rules, rules, rules! About **when** to stand and sit, **where** to stand and sit and **how** to stand and sit.

Families have rules too. Shoulds, should nots, cans and cannots, dos and don'ts.

Here's a Quick Quiz about the rules you remember from your own family life. Fill in the blanks with messages you remember.

This one sounds like "advice".

You shouldn't____

This one is more like an "order".

You mustn't____

Do this and get a "licken".

You'd better not____________________________________

You may also have been told that you ***can't*** do something.

You may have grown up believing that you can't, when in fact, you can.

- Write down a few family rules you agreed with.
- Write down a few rules you thought were unfair!

As children we learn to react. We may accept some of our family expectations and values or we may reject them.

Passive acceptance or angry rejection are two extremes of reaction.

Let's look at a few typical examples of how we may have been conditioned.

Expression of Emotions

Joy, anger, grief and affection are an interesting team of emotions. Some cultures and even some families allow free and open expression of these feelings. How about you – and your family?

THE USE OF MONEY

Have you heard about the "Golden Rule" of money? – "Whoever has the Gold makes the Rules." The control of the cash, bills, investments and how much and where to spend the loot is a very powerful force in a family. How did this work in your family?

PARENTING STYLE

There is a story about a Dad who was able to take pretty well everything in stride. One day he went into his teenage son's room and surveyed the litter of clothes, papers and other "stuff" scattered around the room and hanging on the walls. He finally glanced upward and said, "Son, you sure keep a neat ceiling in your room."

Dad could have exploded in a rage (gone ballistic) and threatened his son with various punishments. Why didn't he? Perhaps he had learned patience from his parents. Perhaps he had been verbally abused by his father or mother and was determined to never treat his children "that way". If so, he would have been unusual or exceptional. Often parents who have been verbally or physically abused as children carry on that tradition of abuse with their own children.

Think about how you were disciplined and punished in your childhood. Whose expectations of behaviour did you follow? Was it fair?

COMMUNICATION STYLE

What did you learn about settling disagreements? Did you grow up in a "my way or the highway" environment? Did your parents avoid confrontation completely?

Or did they teach you to settle agreements and make plans through conversation and compromise?

SOCIAL INVOLVEMENT

How well do you get along with your family?

There are different levels of comfort in how many times people visit with family members and old friends. For example, some are comfortable phoning a parent every day. They may even feel obliged to do so. In other cases there is limited contact. What is your comfort level?

Family Backgrounds, Values and Expectations – Exercise #2, see page 118.

Surprise! No Two People are Alike!

You aren't really surprised, are you? Just head for your nearest shopping mall and watch the people trudging by. Notice the many different faces, sizes and shapes. People have different walking styles. They all talk differently, too!

Try this. Take your shoes off and stand in front of your partner. Check out the differences. O.K., O.K., there are the obvious differences of gender . . . but notice the differences in height, length of fingers, size of foot, colour of hair and eyes and so on.

It should come as no surprise, but it often does, especially for couples in love and newlyweds, that there are deep differences in emotional needs and attitudes as well. These differences are often hidden or denied in the early stages of the relationship. Both partners want everything to be "just right".

The Great Coverup Caper

There may be a fear of jeopardizing the relationship. "I wish he wouldn't swear so much . . . " Or "I wish she/he wouldn't talk on the phone to her sister/mother/friend so much . . . " Nothing is said, however, in an effort to keep the peace.

The marriage relationship, behaviours, sharing responsibilities and emotional and sexual expectations are examples of where greater awareness and mutual understanding will pay off.

The best way to avoid the hidden land mines of the future is by talking, listening, negotiating and cooperating **now**. Work together to discover and disarm these land mines.

Create a greater awareness, a better understanding and acceptance of one another. This can lead to a discovery of the other person's real beauty and humanity.

Love looks
not with the eyes,
but with the mind.
And therefore is wing'd cupid
painted blind"

William Shakespeare

Family Backgrounds, Values and Expectations – Back Handout, see page 119.

Conflict Resolution

Different Styles Of Living Can Create Conflict

The Camping Caper

"We all do things pretty much the same way . . . only differently."

This camping adventure illustrates how:

Conflict, upset and anger can be the result of intolerance of different family practices. Try this wild camping adventure on for size.

Bill, Mary and their son, Jay, are on a weekend camping trip. (No doubt you are thinking that Bill should see a psychiatrist, right? Not at all. Bill is rational and a thoughtfully organized kind of guy.)

Back to the story . . . Bill and Jay go fishing and, like most fishermen, catch nothing but can brag about "the one that got away". To add to the excitement they spotted a bald eagle swooping and diving in the northern sky. Wow! What a thrill!

Meanwhile, back at the ranch, so to speak, things are not going very well. Mary is having a bit of a snit because the tent is not set up and Bill forgot to pack fuel for the camper stove.

Here's the scene. Bill and his trusty sidekick, Jay, make a game of rounding up fire wood. Mary, on the other hand, is fussing and fuming over Bill's lack of organization.

All kinds of dark thoughts are jet screaming through her head. "My Dad always had a comfortable camp set up in no time flat. And he had the meal planned and even prepared well before dark."

Mary and Bill's expectations obviously don't come anywhere near a meeting point.

This bothers Bill. He's a laid-back kind of guy, remember, but becomes a bit irritated over Mary's criticism and demands. He's thinking, "Hey Mary, chill out. Relax and enjoy yourself."

Bill's childhood camping trips, you see, were happy chaotic times, filled with laughter, adventure and excitement. Bill's folks just kind of took things as they came along. No problem.

Whoa, Bill. That's not Mary's cup of camping tea! Somewhere in here we'll have to find a comfort balance in this caper.

Bill, you and Mary take some time around the campfire tonight. You know . . . when Jay has hit the bedroll. Just talk about it . . . Try to understand her frustrations. Tell her about your ideas of camping fun.

Compromise is More Important than Being "Right"

Being "right" about all things is hard work. Such people have taken on an almost God-like status (in their own eyes). What **they** think, say and do is the only way to be.

As a result of this "rightness" they constantly have to defend themselves and their position. They must constantly criticize other opinions or ways of getting things done.

The belief that one way of life or living is superior to another has been the cause of persecution, family turmoil – and raging wars since the beginning of time. Isn't it time to put away the knives and swords of "rightness"?

Limits to Learning

Being right about everything does not allow the individual to learn about others. It is a very limiting way to live what could be an exciting and stimulating life experience.

There is no rule in the Universe that says what your family taught you was absolutely right. They learned from those around them. You can learn from those around you. Take time to explore and accept and compromise with your spouse. Listen to "her" favourite music. Join "him" in a fishing trip.

Forget about all the dos and don'ts – the tiny little rules that we stumble over every day. They really don't matter.

It doesn't matter how he slices the bread . . . It doesn't matter how she cleans the snow off the car . . .

When dealing with yourself – use your head.
When dealing with others – use your heart.

No one can be totally right or totally wrong about most things.

"Nothing in nature is totally right or totally wrong.
That's why it keeps changing."

Balancing – The Tube of Toothpaste

Annette is very methodical about the tube of toothpaste. She uses only a small amount, squeezes it from the bottom and carefully replaces the cap.

Paul squeezes from the middle of the tube, often leaving excess toothpaste on the counter. He rarely puts the cap back on the tube.

This has the potential to be a BIG issue. Or there can be compromise.

- Annette can hassle Paul about his toothpaste procedure and create a daily resentment.
- They can buy several tubes of toothpaste. Green for Annette and white for Paul. They can do whatever they wish with them.
- They can discover that by being more accepting and understanding, the toothpaste issue is really not that big a deal. Paul will try harder not to be so messy. Annette will work at not getting so wound up over such a "small stuff" matter.
- They can grow to realize that should either one of them become seriously ill or injured, the tube of toothpaste issue will become very insignificant, indeed.

  (p.s.: Don't forget to rinse the sink.)

Conflict in Marriage – Differences in Values and Priorities

We all have different values – and different priorities about values. Your judgement and the choices you make on a day-to-day basis are affected by your values.

Have you given your personal values serious thought? What about your spouse's personal values? Do you share a similar value system? That is, are you both able to live with each other's decisions on important issues?

Let's say, for example, that you value loyalty significantly more than honesty. This means that you believe it is quite acceptable to lie for a friend and back the other person no matter what.

How would your spouse feel about living with . . . a liar?

Here's another example. Your spouse may value independence over being known and understood by others (including you). So?

Well, let's say your spouse just doesn't see the point of having to explain why there is a new $2500.00 lawn mower in the garage when the old one was working just fine. Or why it is necessary to phone home to explain some change in plans.

This explaining and "reporting in" is seen as a loss of independence rather than an opportunity to be known and understood.

Could you live a life with someone who was unwilling to communicate in this fashion?

Let's go back to the Camping Caper. How are Bill and Mary getting along? Are they out of the woods yet?

It's obvious that Bill and Mary have expectations that are quite different. Their appreciation of who does what, what ought to happen and how they react are separated by a lack of understanding.

Mary has many fine personal attributes. She happens to value organization, planning and leadership. She has come to expect, through the example of her father, that the man should be in charge.

Now, heeere's Bill. Bill, as we know, is a relaxed, laid-back guy. He values playfulness and adventure more than a finely tuned camp site. He wants to relax, not be the camp leader.

Being the man in charge is not part of his family of origin experience. So it is unlikely he would take on all of Mary's expectations, even if she demanded it of him.

Mary, on the other hand, stands tapping her foot and drumming her fingers, waiting for Bill to get into action. Mary associates fun with a smooth-running organization and having needs met. Hassle-free camping is her goal.

Maybe Mary also believes that more attention should be given to comfort items and meeting basic needs – rather than making the trip into a bit of a wilderness adventure.

What do you think Bill and Mary could learn from each other?

Good Communication and Nurturing Your Relationship – Exercise #1, see page 120.

Basic Ground Rules for Resolving Conflict

Did you ever think about the meaning of the term "ground rules"? It means that you and your partner are on the same level, in the same place and talking about the same thing. Pretty basic to communication but often missed in the heat of an argument.

After 70 years of marriage, an 89-year-old wife explained that she and her 92-year-old husband rarely argued. In the early years of the marriage they were too busy working and raising six children. "Now he is hard of hearing and doesn't hear half of what I say."

When you take on the burden of arguing about ought tos, shoulds and don'ts, simply do what all professional athletes and performers do when facing a stressful situation.

Take a break. Step back, out of the fray. Practice your relaxation breathing, see page 101, for three or four minutes and then come back to resolve the issue using the following ground rules.

Remember how much you love each other.
Remember that you are best friends.
Remember that life is brief and joy is fleeting.
Remember that every healthy relationship is based on self-respect.
Remember that forgiveness is a gift from creation.
Remember to keep your sense of humour.
Remember not to sweat the little things.
Remember to "Never let the sun set on a quarrel".

Conflict Resolution – When and Where

How much time is spent on agonizing over conflicts? Lots. How much time is spent in discussing and resolving these conflicts? Not much.

People will spend hours planning their summer vacation, selecting living room furniture or discussing their golf game. Yet, they are reluctant to dedicate sufficient time to conflict resolution. Perhaps they hope it will just "go away". Well, like the bad golf swing or the ugly furniture, conflicts will not just "go away" either, unless you do something about it. It's important to make the time and take time in your life to meet with your mate and discuss issues, concerns or conflicts.

There are some scenarios to avoid when dealing with conflicts. You and your partner should not enter into discussion of serious issues:

- When you are in a hurry. "Gotta go . . . but remember what I said about the bank overdraft." Zoom . . . "I don't have time to finish this discussion. Stop crying. I'm going to work now. I'll see you at supper time." Slam the door. Zoom . . .
- When you are hungry or are eating. Hungry people tend to be a bit touchy. Discussing vital issues while you are eating may upset your digestive system. Sharing a meal together is a time of communion and for the enjoyment of the gifts of creation.
- When you are tired. Fatigue taxes the brain. Your thinking ability is suppressed. Late night is not the time to roll out the "big bowling ball" subjects for your mate to dodge.
- Bedtime is a good time to visit, cuddle and be close. You don't want to be like the fellow who was just slipping off to dreamland when his wife tapped him on the shoulder and said, "By the way, honey, someone from Revenue Canada called you this afternoon. Good night, dear."
- When you could be constantly interrupted or are in a public place. Raging children, telephone interruptions or getting up to check the barbecue are not good scenarios for a serious discussion. Neither is a restaurant. You and your partner cannot allow your emotions comfortable rein in a public place.

Right, there is no "perfect" time or place. The following steps, however, will help you set the stage for productive discussion.

- Agree on a subject.
- Agree on a time – and a time limit.
- Agree on a place of comfort.
- Agree to come to some form of resolution before ending your discussion, even if it is just to agree to disagree AND discuss it further at a later time.

Resolving Conflict in a Relationship

The BRAIN is a marvellous instrument. While it has no nerves, it is the source of many feelings. There is a section in the frontal lobe of the brain that is the base of our human survival mechanism.

When our prehistoric ancestors were under severe threat (attack by a sabre-toothed tiger) this portion of the brain would go into a "flight (take-off, eh) or fight (slug-it-out)" mode.

This protective function still kicks in when we are threatened, as in a heated argument. There is a tremendous rush of adrenaline which makes us physically stronger – and there is an absence of rational thought. We operate on "remote control". The thinking part of our brain actually shuts down as we go into a survival mode.

Thus when two people are shouting and arguing with each other, they are both physically highly energized by the adrenaline – and essentially BRAIN DEAD.

You may have noticed this when two people are arguing. They are often yelling about two different things, getting red in the face, waving their arms and sputtering at each other. It would be funny if it wasn't so hurtful.

Here are some basic communication rules that will help avoid aggressive and hurtful arguing.

As your friend and loving companion I ask you to:

- Not yell at me.
- Not swear at me.
- Not invade my personal space (physical, mental, emotional, spiritual space).

I agree to respect you in the same manner.

These fundamental rules will move your discussion from Confrontation to Conversation.

Taking Sides

Often one partner will accuse the other of "taking sides". This is usually a defence mechanism used to score points. Having an opinion and expressing it is not "taking sides". Opinions are formed of an individual's own free will and may not concur with your partner's.

If you accuse your partner of taking sides, then so are you!

Good Communication and Nurturing Your Relationship – Exercise #2, see page 121.

Steps on the Journey to Resolving Conflict

Stay on the Path – Keep to the Here and Now

The biggest problem with human beings is our memory. We remember too much from the past. We may not keep track of where we spend our money, but we keep an accurate accounting of who did what – and said what – on what day – and in what place.

This is called SANDBAGGING. We drag along these bags of sand just in case we need them for ammunition. They also help us feel sorry for ourselves as we remember past hurts. Those bags sure get heavy, don't they?

Then there are the wounding arrow words – "you never" and "you always". These words usually make the situation unsolvable. They not only drag up the past but provide ammunition for your partner, such as:

Sending Arrow

"You're always late for supper and you never phone to tell me."

Returning Arrow

"What! I'm not always late for supper. I was only late 12 times in the last month. (Some people do keep track.) And I distinctly remember calling you at least 7 of those 12 times . . . etc. . . . etc. . . ."

It's best to keep your discussion to the present moment. That is, state the problem and how you can work together to solve it.

Keep to One Issue

"Darling, I'd like to talk to you about our budget. It seems that you've overspent a bit on your golf equipment . . . "

"Oh, yeah! Well what about that time last year when you bought all those Barry Manilow CDs! You didn't hear me complaining . . . and besides, why do you never put the milk back in the refrigerator . . . ?

Some people keep a job jar (or list) in the kitchen to determine what has to be done around the house or apartment. Similarly, you could make a list of the things in your relationship that have to be resolved. Write each item on a separate piece of paper. Review them and decide which ONE you wish to discuss. You may find that other item(s) are related. If so, bring that one into the discussion.

Do not bring in other issues because of a need to protect yourself, to defeat the other's argument or to equalize the conflict.

"Remember that the purpose of your discussion is not to start or win a battle, but to learn how to get along."

Avoid Character Attacks

For some, resolving conflicts often means "I have to win – or at least come out even". In this case people bring in the heavy guns of character assassination or "name calling".

Perhaps you or your partner behaved irresponsibly or did a – well, a stupid thing. This doesn't mean that the person is irresponsible or stupid.

Keep your comments to the **behaviour** in question rather than belittling the person or making judgemental statements.

Belittling Statement: Expressing annoyance, anger

"You know Walter, you are really stupid. Why are you even thinking of buying that wreck of a car?"

Behaviour Statement: Expressing concern, care

"Walter, honey, I am really concerned about that car you are looking at. I feel that you may be into some long-term repairs . . . "

Which one would **you** rather hear?

"Do you love the snorer, but not the snoring?" This is a good example of how we can separate the individual's personal qualities from his or her behaviour.

Name Calling is a No-No!

Example:

"Boy, are you ever a DUMBBELL."

"Me, a dumbbell? Why you're nothing but a !$#@ !@#$!%&*(!"

"You can't call me that you *()$^& @$%%^$ %&^@#$%!"

"Oh, yeah, you @$%%^&*(#$%^$%@#$% $^%(@#$%^& %$*&!"

Name calling is hurtful and very counter productive. It gets in the way of real communication. It goes to the centre of one's personal self-worth. As you can see, and as you may have heard, it often tends to expand and even move into physical attack.

> ***"The Inuit have fifty-two names for snow because it is important to them. There ought to be as many for love."***
>
> *paraphrasing* Margaret Atwood

Do Not Counter Attack

As we saw in the name-calling example, counter attack is also counter productive.

Conflict resolution is a matter of building bridges – not competing to see who can get more angry, more hurt or more righteous.

Use your listening skills, page 52. Try to accept that the other person has the right to be upset even if they have done things to hurt you. Reacting with similar or greater force of emotion will simply step up the conflict.

Take a break. Step back. Step out of the circle. Do relaxation breathing. Speak without yelling.

Avoid Mind Reading

No one can tell what another person is thinking, feeling or wanting. Nor can they tell about you! So, don't try to interpret your spouse's behaviour, words, facial expressions or body language. Their attitudes and motives are also beyond your mind-reading skills.

Better to stick to reading your own mind. You are an expert only about **yourself**.

Avoid Trying to Succeed

Conflict resolution is discussion to achieve a mutually satisfactory goal. You are not coaching in the World Series or Olympic finals. Avoid creating a mental game plan that says your spouse must: understand your viewpoint, back down, give in or choose your way. Such an approach will result in hostility and failure.

Your spouse will gain trust in the process when you go for: listening, settling with what you can live with, what you have in common and on what you can compromise together.

Use "I" Messages

Hit the rewind button on your past conversations tape and you may hear sentence starters like these:

"You should have . . . Why didn't you . . . You make me . . . "

"You" statements lead to defensiveness. "I" statements, however, are gestures of caring and concern. In most cases they will evoke a listening rather than a defending response.

Here are some "You versus I" examples:

"You should have told me you were going to be late!"

or

"I would really appreciate knowing when you are going to be late. I get very concerned when I don't hear from you."

"Why do you always forget to buy my favourite kind of cheese?"

or

"Honey, I know you like to try different kinds of cheese, but I would prefer some of my favourite Cheddar next time."

"You make me feel very angry when you leave all the dishes in the sink."

or

"Darling, I would like you to take a few extra minutes to clear the dishes out of the sink."

Resolving Conflict – Learning to Forgive and Forget

"I can't forgive. I can't forget." The truth is you can forgive and you can forget. You have decided that you **won't**. Decide that you will. And then do.

Everyone has the ability to move into forgiveness – to let things go . . . to stop reminding ourselves of misdeeds, misfortunes and so-called mistakes.

Time, in its healing, will allow the issue or incident to fade. Something we thought we could never forgive or forget will become difficult to remember. Eventually, if we allow it, the memory will become like a faded photo from the past. The features so blurred that we cannot make out who is in the picture. Well, there's no sense keeping a photo like that.

On the other hand, remembering and recalling an incident or issue serves only to reinforce it in our memory. The angst, anger, sorrow, grief, disappointment and other debilitating conditions will only be strengthened. Like getting the photo touched up every once in a while, to remind ourselves and others, just to make sure the memory stays fresh. We also make photocopies and store them in the drawer to look at. We make extra copies to pass around.

What fun is it to collect ugly pictures and even pass them around for others to see? There are greater things to do and to think about in our brief time in this life cycle. There are things for us to be and then to do. There are many greater needs than to keep regurgitating painful and uncomfortable memories.

Retaining bitter memories creates a continuing bitterness in our lives. This feeling, however well we try to hide it, will affect every thought and action in some way. Your spouse, children, family and friends will be affected by how you feel about some long-past incident.

Give yourself permission to let the memories fade away. Keep only the jewels. Let the sands of anger, regret and disappointment slip through your fingers and into the wind.

"Write kindness in marble and injuries in the dust."
Persian Proverb

Family Backgrounds, Values and Expectations – Handout, see page 125.

Communication

Good Communication And Nurturing Your Relationship

Communication is Giving and Receiving

Like a teeter-totter. A nice, comfortable balance of give and take – and no one gets hurt.

Communication is the process whereby two or more people actively give and receive information from one another.

Communication is talking and listening. It is paying attention and acknowledging the other person. It works when it is mutual. That is, both partners actively talk and listen to each other with respect.

It doesn't work when the teeter-totter is out of balance or when one person jumps off.

The Message has Both Content and Meaning

The content is about what's going on (the environment), the self (that's you) or the other person.

What's meaning? It's a mix of messages. A complex blending of feelings, needs, beliefs and opinions. Each person's past experiences, fears, reservations and expectations are mixed into the discussion.

For example, let's use a simple statement such as:

> *"Ahem, Mary/John. There is only twenty dollars left in the chequing account!"*

The next message could be expressed as an **expectation of needs**:

> *"I thought there was more money left in the account because I hadn't written any cheques, and I needed to pay for the car repairs today."*

Another message could **convey feelings**:

> *"What the hell is going on with the money. Why was there only twenty dollars left?!!!"*

The message could also convey **one's values, biases and beliefs:**

> *"I feel it is important to pay for my car repairs right away. I feel embarrassed when I write a cheque that is going to be NSF!"*

It can also convey the **desire to have power over the other person**:

> *"Why didn't you tell me you spent all the money? What is wrong with you? Don't you ever do this again!"*

No doubt you've experienced a situation where you told someone something and they totally misunderstood or misinterpreted what you **thought** you said.

Perhaps you weren't making yourself clear. Perhaps the other person was away in "la-la land" while you spoke.

It is more likely that the filters got in the way. Filters? Yes, the filters called feelings, conditioning and habits which can affect the content and meaning of the message.

Imagine yourself wearing a thin curtain that changes what you intend to say. And imagine your listener wearing a similar curtain. The message is getting through but the meaning is not.

Remove the screen by making it clear what you intend to achieve with your message.

Do you intend to explain something, to control something, to confront something, or to reconcile something?

Make your intent clear to yourself first and then to your partner. Look around. There are no Swamis in the household. Your partner cannot read your mind. Unless you state your intentions, the only way your partner can discover your intent is to either ask you directly or to take a guess at it, by how and what you send as a message.

How You Say Something – The Other Half of the Message

Pardon the incorrect English but there's an old saying that goes, "It ain't **watcha** say, it's the **way** that ya say it!" Whatever the grammar, the message is clear.

The first half of the message is content and meaning.

The second half is **how** you say it.

Sure, the message can be sent from your data centre (brain) with words. But the words are accompanied and embellished by your feelings, posture, facial expressions, gestures or even through silence.

Yes, it is possible to send a message through silence. Sitting alone in a corner with your arms folded and not saying anything works. Any pouting child knows how powerful this message can be.

Let's look at how our mood can influence the message. For example, when you are in a bad mood, a gruff statement such as, "Where's the paper?" can lead to upset or even an argument. Think back over the times when you or members of your family got into conflict over such a situation.

Try the same message sent without the sharp edges of gruffness. "Where's the paper, honey?" (There's that sweet word, again.) This good mood message sent with feeling, body posture, facial expressions (smile) and gestures (hug) will convey your good mood. It will lead to an open, non-defensive and warm exchange with your spouse.

Try this Word-Meaning Experiment:

Say: "I DIDN'T SAY HE STOLE THE MONEY!"

Now say it with emphasis on one word. Emphasize the word "I". Then say it again emphasizing the word "DIDN'T" and so on. Notice how the meaning changes with every change in emphasis!

"Pleasant words are a honeycomb,
Sweet to the soul and healing to the bones."
Proverbs 16:24

Besides, who wants to be a grouch, anyway? You have to keep remembering what you are grouchy about and with whom you are grouchy. Whew! Hard Work! Take a break. De-grouch yourself.

There's more! Another angle to this communication process is called Mixed Messages. This occurs when the **words** do not match appropriately with the **intent** or the **way** it is sent. (Like a politician promising increased spending and lower taxes. Huh?)

Picture this mixed message. You say, "I'm not angry, only hurt!" Sure, we believe you. NOT! Look at your body language. Your hands are clenched. You are talking through your teeth – like a ventriloquist. Your eyes – you are glaring. Wow! What a mixed message!

Yes, the **body and feelings** convey anger. Yes, the **words** convey denial of anger and emphasize hurt. What do we believe?

Other Mixed Messages to watch out for:

You say "yes" when you really mean "no". Your lips move and you speak the word "yes" while your body language and feelings scream "NO!" A bit confusing. Yes? No?

You say that you want to solve a problem with your mate and instead you launch into a personal attack and pick an argument. Confusing and upsetting.

Listening – The Other Half of Communication

Go stand on a high hill all by yourself. Shout out what it is you have to say and then go home. Great! You sent the message but nobody was listening. Isn't it frustrating when people don't listen?

Sending needs receiving. It's the other half of the equation. It's the cone for the ice cream . . . the pail for the water . . .

Good listeners are attentive, considerate, polite and interested people. How do you measure up? Excuse me, did you hear the question?

Courtesy Pays

Being a good listener means using a few simple techniques or "tricks". Really, it's just plain courtesy.

Make eye contact, show interest (emotional openness) and focus your attention on the speaker. Avoid going overboard. Just **be** and **act** interested or concerned.

As a good and effective listener you will try to make sure the message is understood. You try to avoid filling in the gaps or guessing about the speaker's motivation, intentions or feelings. You suspend judgements or opinions. You do not spend your listening time trying to make up responses. You wait until the speaker has completed the message. You do not interrupt.

The KEY that opens the door to successful communication is making sure that the listener (receiver) has the same understanding of the content and meaning as does the sender (speaker).

Doesn't it feel great when some one actually **listens** to you and **acknowledges** you?

Do This at Home!

See what it's really like to have a good listener. Talk to your dog, cat, budgie, plant – whatever. They are non-judgemental and will give you full attention. Except the dog that will leave you in a fit of barking when the door bell rings.

Listening carefully to another person demonstrates respect, positive regard, interest and caring.

It encourages open communication with your mate.

Try this line: "Go ahead. I'm interested in what you have to say."

Listening Hints:

"God gave us two ears and one mouth so that we should listen twice as much as we talk."

Anonymous

It is estimated that we spend nearly half of our waking hours listening – yet our efficiency rate is only 25 per cent.

"When we are listened to it creates us, makes us unfold and expand. Ideas actually begin to grow within us and come to life."

Brenda Ueland

"You are a nice person but you talk too much with your mouth."

as told to Cuthbert McNiel

Healthy Communication is a Learned Behaviour

Can you do this? Can you tie your shoelaces or button a shirt without looking at the laces or buttons – **while** you are talking to someone? Can you play cards, a musical instrument or drive a car?

These are learned behaviours. Think of other ordinary things you do that are learned behaviours. Things we can do without really thinking. (Remember the time you drove for 30 kilometres and had no recollection?)

It's the same thing with communication. Sure, genetics have some influence, but healthy communication skills are simply learned behaviours which become good habits. Like learning to play a game or musical instrument – it takes practice. Both partners in a relationship have to practice – practice – practice.

Your Serve, LOVE!

Here's an example. Try playing tennis with a partner who refuses to participate. You whack the ball and your "chum" just stands there.

No reaction. No action. Same thing with communication. It takes two!

When you are both in the game each person takes a turn, in sequence, hitting the ball so the other person can hit it back. Fire a blistering overhand and your partner will be hurt and will lose trust in you. Start whacking in a whole pail of balls and your partner doesn't know which one to send back to you. Get the idea?

Poor communication is like an extremely competitive tennis match. No referees and a thousand balls in the court. Each opponent is trying to outwit, outmanoeuvre and trash the other.

Win! Win! Win! Win what? You may have won the argument but you've lost BIG TIME in communicating with your best friend. You **are** best friends, remember?

Play fair. Play with one ball. Let each other know it is coming. A nice gentle underhand. Encourage and compliment each other. "Nice return, darling!"

Once you get the hang of it with one ball, you may be able to use two or more. Just like a couple of jugglers. Team work, practice, patience . . . WOW! What great communicators.

> ***"When a woman is upset, keep quiet." Advice from a 103-year-old Schenectady, New York, resident Edmund Sobieski, who celebrated his 80th wedding anniversary with his 100-year-old wife, Genevieve, in January 1997.***
>
> Source: *NEWSWEEK January 20, 1997*

The BIG Seven Communication Skills

Only seven? Well, sure there are lots of things to consider but the Big Seven will set the foundation for you and your partner. The Big Seven will also help you in your communications with other people in your life. Your children, family, friends, the nice lady at the grocery store, the folks where you work . . . all kinds of magnificent opportunities.

By practicing these skills, your marriage and your LIFE will become more vital, interesting and healthy.

1. Be direct and clear.

State your point. Say what you mean and not what you think the other person wants to hear. Speak directly about issues (what's troubling you), feelings (anger, excitement, disappointment, joy).

Camouflaging or dressing them up will only disguise the real concern.

If you want to know, ask. Sounds simple but millions of people are held back because they didn't muster up the courage to ask the question. Seek information you really wish to know. Ask about something you really do not know the answer to. It's O.K. to say "I don't know" rather than trying to cover up or play manipulation games.

2. Name your feelings while expressing them.

Let 'er rip. When you are angry, don't just YELL!!!. Put words into your feelings. Say, "I'm so angry, I could yell!" There, feel better? By naming your feelings, you will have given yourself and others a clear message. Your intentions will be more evident and you will have better self-control.

3. Use "I" messages rather than "You" messages.

Hang in with us here. As when you first learned how to do long division or program your VCR, it may seem complicated at first.

Here's the scenario. Something is burning in your brain. You want to tell your spouse without recreating the Halifax Explosion, the Frank Slide and the Red River Flood of '97 – all at once.

It's important to describe your needs, feelings and interpretations and not blame the other person for some perceived wrong doing.

Here's how it works. When you say "You are stupid!", you are insulting the other person's integrity. Indeed, they may have done a very stupid thing. They may have acted in a foolish or irresponsible manner. But they are not stupid!

It would serve the world well if we were to eliminate the word "stupid" from our vocabulary.

You can avoid offending your mate by using "I" statements such as: "I feel very angry about what you did. That was a very thoughtless thing to do." Or: "I am so frustrated by what you did that I could just scream!"

"I" messages are less offensive and tend to open the door to listening and negotiating. It's scary to be under attack. Being under attack creates fear and a loss of trust.

"I" messages are great for asking for what you need, rather than complaining, nagging or putting the other person down.

The Golden Rule of Communication – Do No Harm

4. Check Out Your Interpretation and Understanding.

This is called "Reflecting". Just like a mirror, you reflect back what the other person is saying to be sure you are getting it right – or that they are saying what they really want to say.

Remember, you are not a Swami/Mind Reader. Neither is your partner.

Mind reading takes the form of jumping to conclusions or using past assumptions. Why not check out your interpretation and understanding about what was just said?

Reflecting asks for clarification. "Honey, I want to be sure I understand that what you are saying is . . . " These questions will help guide the conversation, explain things you don't understand and recapture ideas you may have missed.

5. Keep to One Issue.

Like in the tennis game – play with one ball at a time. When your partner says something that reminds you of an unrelated idea, stifle the desire to express it.

Avoid dragging in other people, whether they are there or not. "Larry, tell Mary about how much better it would be if . . . " or "Joan told me that she heard you say . . . "

Keep the topic and the goal in mind and work to stay on track.

When you both feel comfortable about having come to an agreement, summarize your agreement. Then shake hands . . . O.K., that's too formal. How about a hug to seal the deal?

6. Show Positive Regard. (I love you. I respect you. I trust you.)

What really bugs you about conversing with your mate? Does he or she interrupt, finish your sentences for you, drift off, get angry, swear – or even snore? What is your rating of yourself in these categories?

Positive regard means respecting the other person's feelings, opinions, needs and individuality. Give respect and you'll get respect. Not showing positive regard will cause a breakdown in your communication.

7. Be An Active Listener.

"Go, ahead, I'm listening" are very encouraging words. They mean that you are an **active** listener. Keep appropriate eye contact but remember this is not a staring contest. Recheck (reflect) the message being conveyed and give some feedback along the way.

Avoid waiting for the other person to pause or take a breath so you can "jump in" (another form of interrupting).

Give your partner subtle signs of encouragement. Nod your head and acknowledge what they say with "ahas", "I sees" and "mmhmms".

BONUS NUMBER:

8. Mind Your Body Language.

Body language makes up a big part of the message. Your posture, facial expressions, voice tone and eye contact all influence how willing you are to communicate.

Imagine, for example, someone slouched in a chair with their arms folded across their chest and their face set in a scowl. What kind of a communicator do we have here? Not a pretty sight!

Good Communication Nurtures Your Marital Relationship

Terrific marriages are not made in the stars. They are the result of love based on honesty, trust, honour, communication – and hard work!

The success of your relationship will be affected by what you put into it. Imagine that you have planted an apple tree. Your goal is to ensure that the tree grows to eventually produce juicy sweet-tasting apples.

In order to get the fruit, you both must care for and nurture the little tree. Water it, stake it against the winds and protect it from insect and animal pests. You will have to prune, spray and fertilize your little tree. Thus it will grow those juicy apples.

Some branches will have to be supported. Some diseased branches will have to be removed.

So it is with your relationship. Your relationship is the tree you plant and work on together to help it grow. Your relationship will give back what you put into it. Cultivate and care for your "tree" with good communications, loving care and a generous measure of forgiveness. Then enjoy the delicious fruit of your efforts! Bon appetit!

Yackity-Yack – There is More than One Way of Talking

So far . . . we have learned about the basics of communication through talking and listening. Now we can fine tune our skills through the following tips on talking.

- **Informing:** Straightforward information sharing for organizing, planning, decision making and understanding things.

  "I will be home at 5:30 and after supper we can go shopping."

- **Sharing:** These are private times. Gentle times of talking about each other's personal world of memories, dreams, hopes, joys, expectations and needs.

  "Remember our first vacation together? I'll never forget the time you bought me that beautiful . . . "

- **Affirming:** Here you can give each other credit for positive attributes, appreciate each other's talents, skills and good efforts. Offer emotional support in times of need. A shoulder to lean on or perhaps to cry on.

  "Darling, I really appreciate the way you comforted me when . . . "

- **Confronting:** Do this to clear the air, but not in an unkind or harsh manner. Agree to talk about those things that you would rather hide away. Issues, situations, behaviours and needs. The things that affect you, the relationship, the children or the family directly. Opening the windows on these issues will bring in fresh air.

  "I feel it is important that we settle the issue of . . . now. I am willing to spend whatever time it takes. We cannot let this go on any longer."

- **Negotiating:** There is a situation that needs to be resolved. Talk it over in the spirit of compromise. Discuss alternatives, consequences and outcomes. Who will be affected and in what way? Is it beneficial to all concerned?

  An important part of negotiating is compromise. Give a little and take a little. In the end ask yourself, "Can I live with it?"

- **Forgiving:** Who among us does not need to be forgiven? Forgiving is an expression of love, trust and honour from the heart. Forgiveness helps mend broken hearts, comforts bruised egos, cultivates hope and builds bridges of trust. Forgiving means forgetting. Not dragging up hurts and harms from the past. Tough work but well worth the effort.

"How sweet the words, 'I forgive you'. Word gifts of forgiveness – so soothing to the heart and soul."

Anonymous

- **Lovemaking:** Express your affection, passion and pleasure for one another. Talk about each other's needs and comforts. Lovemaking also includes subtle messages. A loving look from across the room, a little hug or pat, a surprise phone call, and comforting words. "Honey dos" are loving deeds we do for each other.

These seven types of talking will help you grow that beautiful tree of mutual love and respect. Both of you and everyone around will share in the bounty of your efforts.

Create a balance in using these skills. Focusing on one or two skills to the exclusion of others will cause the relationship to become stagnant or burdensome.

Use all of these skills to maintain more vitality and energy and openness in your relationship. You and your spouse will grow as individuals as well as life partners.

Sabotage: Your relationship will be threatened by many outside sources. A healthy relationship will guard against and deal with such threats. Sabotage from inside sources is more destructive and hurtful. Be thoughtful, caring and considerate. Do not launch torpedoes at your own boat.

"Temper gets you into trouble. Pride keeps you there."

Anonymous

Good Communication and Nurturing Your Relationship – Exercise #3, see page 124.

Sexual Intimacy

Sexuality Is Our Humanness

SEX! It's everywhere! Television, magazines, billboards and advertising. It's like it was just invented! Billions of dollars are spent using sexual appeal to sell everything from cars to computers, booze to bowling balls and of course, sex itself! Sex is the theme for movies, television dramas, the soaps, books and live entertainment.

People laugh about it, tell jokes about it, cry over it, seek medical attention about it, argue over it and even use it as a weapon in relationships.

Sex is big business in our secular society. For some it is a recreation, a distraction or entertainment. For others it is a basic biological need like eating, sleeping and voiding.

Sex can be very good or very bad. It can hurt or heal.

Let's explore the various dimensions of sexuality and sex, and what impact they have on our individual lives and relationship with others.

God is for our Humanness

Sexuality is a human experience.

Sexuality to the Christian is not body versus spirit, lust versus holiness or even evil versus good. There is a belief in the secular community that God punished Adam and Eve by casting them out of paradise because of the hanky panky of sexual sins.

The informed Christian is aware that mind and body are loved by God in unity. Otherwise, why would the resurrection from the dead and the ascension of Christ's physical presence be of significance to us?

God's love for our humanity is revealed throughout the scriptures. This is love as a motherly, fatherly and sensual appreciation of our humanity. We are made in God's image and likeness.

Our sexuality is sacred.
It is our humanness.
God is in favour of our humanness.

Sharing our Sexuality

Sexuality is more than "the body in motion". It is our physical and psychological femaleness and maleness. Every individual has the choice of how to express their sexuality. It is not up to nature, society or your partner to determine how you will express your sexuality.

"It's your free choice" as to how much importance you give to sexual intimacy in your life and how you express it. You are the one who decides how you control and explore your sexual urges. No one else can make these decisions for you.

Sexual Intimacy – Exercise #1, see page 109.

Two Major Misunderstandings About Sexuality

Let's Do "IT"

Sex is not an "it" outside of an individual's control. It is a sense. A spiritual and emotional union with the physical being. Sex and sexuality are powerful forces yet they cannot be put into a container, weighed and sent off to another town.

Sexual intimacy, at whatever level, is a giving and sharing of yourself with mutual love and respect. This intimacy is not an "it". Your maleness and femaleness form a bond of sensual experience physically, emotionally – and spiritually.

Those who see sex and sexuality simply as an "it" or a "thing to do" find themselves as spectators in the act of making love.

Sex is only Genital Activity

Wait a minute! There has to be more to great sex than that! How about those communication techniques we discussed earlier? Same with sexuality. Give and receive with mutual respect. Same as a good conversation, right? Well, maybe not quite the same!!!

Being intimate with your partner is a communication of tenderness, stimulation, excitement and satisfaction. Your verbal and physical messages convey love, tenderness and a general willingness to make your partner "feel good all over" – physically and emotionally.

For most men – it's great sex first and "feel good" conversation after. For women – it's verbal and emotional intimacy (take your time) first and then the enjoyment of giving and receiving love while being sexually intimate.

An awareness and blending of these needs will help create a fulfilling sexual relationship for both partners.

Healthy, Balanced Sexual Relationships Take Time

Sexual "experience" for some is a point of personal achievement. The number of times they have had sex with others is presented as if they were in some sort of athletic competition. They know technique and have the style. None of these points have much to do with healthy, happy conjugal love.

It is important to allow yourself and your partner time. Time for your love and lovemaking to grow in a healthy and vital way. Time gives you the opportunity to really get to know yourself and your mate.

Take that time to learn about your own and your mate's subtleties and sensitivities. We are complex beings. There are all kinds of little nooks and crannies in our psychological, emotional and physical beings.

"Getting to Know You . . . "

Get to know each other. Talk about and discover each other's sensitivities, sexual responsiveness, needs and preferences. People talk about their preferences in food, entertainment and recreation. Why not talk as openly about your sexual intimacy?

In some cases, there may be some ancient stumbling blocks in the way. Something left over from a past experience. A personal fear, trauma or taboo. Take time. Be gentle in expressing yourself.

Learn to express and receive your spouse's affections by telling or showing what enhances your intimacy. This way you can eliminate or at least reduce hurt feelings produced by playing the guessing game.

"I wonder if she would enjoy it if . . . ? I wish he would . . . "

We cannot assume what our partner likes or dislikes. Check it out. Bring in your communication skills. Ask. Thus you can avoid falling into a repetitious ritual in this wondrous act of sexual intimacy and loving communication.

How long does it take? As long as it takes. There is no deadline. The learning is continuous.

Sexual Intimacy – Exercise #2 and #3, see page 115.

The Cycles of Romance & Marriage

Growth Means Change

Look around you. Everything in nature is cyclical. The Earth goes around the sun. The seasons change in a regular pattern. Cycles in life are a natural and somewhat predictable force.

These cycles or phases also affect our relationships with ourselves and with others. The rhythm of change affects how you react and interact. Being aware of these forces will help you adjust to the changes you will face in your relationship over the years.

"The only permanent thing is change."

Consider all the changes that a new relationship can bring into your life. Falling in love, for example, can be a very stressful experience. There are two internal forces at work. One is the longing for all the "cuddly comforts" of new love – acceptance, acknowledgement and sharing mutual interests are some of the benefits. There is also a protective force chugging away. This force reminds you about how you might become hurt in the relationship. Balancing these two forces will help you recognize both the dangers and delights of your relationship.

The Romance Phase – Infatuation*

In this phase the relationship has just begun to take shape. The Romance Phase of the relationship is a time to discover your similarities and differences. A time to determine if you really want to be lifetime partners by **mutual choice**!

It is an exciting, tantalizing time.It holds out the promise that this will be "THE" relationship. The one that will make the difference in your life. You may look upon this exciting time as proof that the relationship is the "be-all and end-all". It will solve all your problems and be a replacement for everything you don't have and don't like about your life.

"Wow! Everything about him/her is so great!!"

There are great releases of physical and emotional energy. The newness and the excitement of discovery in the unknown becomes sexually arousing. You laugh about your differences and revel in your common interests.

"We both like this and that and we both had pet turtles when we were kids."

You risk involvement, relate personal information and make promises. The passion for one another is enhanced. This focus of energy gives life new meaning and overrides all other relationships. The promise of a happy and fulfilling life may be attained. The world, indeed, is a wondrous place.

Infatuation sets in. Emotions are overpowering. Nothing can be or can go wrong. You can't concentrate. You jump up onto cloud nine and go sailing around in ecstasy. Infatuation, though, even with all its power, is not love. It could be the first step toward love but it is not, in itself, true love.

* The material for the cycles of romance and marriage is taken with permission from *Between the Sexes* by Judy and James Sellner, Self Counsel Press, 1987.

The Early Commitment Phase

Take the time and give the energy that will solidify your relationship. You are preparing for a lifelong journey.

Thus, the Early Commitment phase is the time to bond to one another psychologically and interpersonally. Admit it. You are no longer single. You cannot expect to have the same freedoms of being and doing what you were before.

"What do you mean, you're going out with . . . on Saturday? I thought we would . . ."

You will have to make constant adjustments in this new relationship with your best friend. Every decision you make will affect the other person significantly and immediately.

Rely on your intuition when evaluating an intimate relationship.

Do you feel safe just being who you are in this relationship? Do you feel safe being with this person?

The Awareness Session

Now is a good time to learn about each other's very ordinary human qualities and quirks. "He doesn't like his toast buttered while it's hot. She doesn't like it when he goes around the house without a shirt on." More than learning about these minor irritations, you can use this time of discovery to share common interests, common activities, common hopes and attitudes. You will learn that you can learn from each other. There will be plenty of opportunities for you to be patient and understanding. You can also learn that there are times to just accept some things and leave them just as they are.

"Don't sweat the small stuff." (P.S. It's all small stuff.)

You now have new goals as you prepare for your life journey together. Blending your individual lives also includes blending with each other's circle of family, friends, personal interests and work.

This is the best time to be open; let go of old habits; establish new bonds of love, appreciation and understanding for each other.

"Love is willing to enter into the heart, as light is willing to flood a room with windows opened to its brightness."

Anonymous

Now is when the initial familiarity and excited sense of belonging to "someone" will energize your sexual interests and pleasures. You explore and revel in one another's similarities. Lots of phone calls, long distance bills, loving calls from the office, looong lunches and cosy times together.

There is, however, the reality of – reality. As you become more familiar with each other, the excitement is diminished. Like the first time driving through the mountains. "Wow! Look at that . . . and that!" After a few trips, people hardly pay attention to the majesty and dramatic scenery. "Been there, done that . . . " is a common expression of familiarity.

The mystery and fascination diminish. The image you have of your "perfect partner" becomes more difficult to sustain. They, after all, are not perfect. Who is? You begin to notice this and that about your partner's personality and behaviour. What was once cute and worth chuckling over now becomes a source of minor irritation.

"Why does he always show up late? . . . Why does she keep saying these things about her family . . . ?"

The result? A drop in verbal communication and sexual interest. Over familiarity or even boredom can be a real possibility at this time.

The Conflict/Power Struggle Phase

Becoming familiar with someone or something is OK. It allows us to have a sense of knowing what to expect. What would happen, for example if the street names in your community were changed every other week? Confusion, frustration and even anger would be the result. And all those pizzas would never get delivered on time!

There are things about your relationship that also must remain fundamentally unchanged. Love, honour and trust are a few. Day-to-day familiarity, however, can lead to each person discovering the other's mundane, petty, predictable and even selfish side.

"I didn't know she/he felt that way about . . . !"

Pop! The bubbles of the so-called "perfect" relationship have burst. Alas, the billowy dreams of the "perfect" mate have evaporated as he continues to leave his clothing on the bedroom floor or she spends hours on the phone talking to her mother.

The next step is plain old disillusionment about the relationship. It becomes so easy to start making comparisons. You become judgemental and defensive when you are disillusioned. Now you can easily slip into focusing on your differences rather than all the things you have in common. (Remember how nice it was in the Romance Phase?)

Somehow your partner's interests, needs, values, habits and expectations compete – or even contradict your own. A sure sign of a break in the dam is less forgiveness and understanding. Likes and dislikes begin to clash. Conflicts begin to increase in frequency, duration and intensity.

"A tiny stone in the shoe can cause irritation. Best not to curse the stone or the shoe, but to pause and remove the stone."

Anonymous

Here are some signs of conflict (power struggles, leaky dams).

Check off the ones that apply to you (not your partner).

Being overly __angry, __argumentative

__pouting, __withdrawing, ___silence (ooh, that's a good one)

__jealousy, __yelling, __slamming doors

Intentionally __being late, or __forgetting arrangements

__withholding sexual intimacy, __being "nice" (like syrup)

__always doing things with family and friends

__avoiding one another, __nagging ('round and 'round)

__lecturing one another (acting like parents, not friends)

Firing off __put downs, __sarcasms

__ __ __ any others you may wish to add.

At this point in the relationship it is vital that the partners step back and re-evaluate. Remember your loving commitment to each other. You are best friends. Would you do any of the above to your best friend? Probably not.

Understand that you are learning about each other's differences. Yet you are united in your common love, honour and trust. Your common roles, rules, feelings and expectations are still the foundation for your relationship. It is a natural process for you to be in some degree of conflict as you find your way through the maze of learning and accepting one another's differences. You can choose to accept, forgive wrong doings and work at problem solving.

You can choose to work at negotiating mutually acceptable plans. It is your choice.

"Change your power STRUGGLES into power SNUGGLES."

Conflict in Lovemaking: "Let's make love . . . No, let's not!" It should come as no surprise that these times of conflict and adjustment affect how often and why couples make love.

He wants to and she doesn't. Or vice versa. One is either not interested or available. Or at least that is what they **say**. What a difference from the Romance Days! Everything seems "out of sync". Some couples get into raging battles, make up and really get into their sexual intimacy. Others just give in. "Oh well, might as well get it over with!" They become indifferent and disinterested.

Others seem to feed off the arguing and fighting and become dependent on it for sexual arousal. Others use love making as sexual favours that are handed out for "good behaviour". Lovemaking becomes a bargaining tool or used as a reward.

Losin' the Lovin'

Conjugal lovemaking can become a point of disillusionment. The relationship struggles through the stormy seas of learning and growing. Many people seek to compensate for this by over-valuing work, children, the extended family, recreation, money, friends and so on.

"More time jogging, another drink, another couple of hours at work, another round of golf, more time with my friends. Anything to avoid confronting this 'sex thing'."

Learning to overcome the conflicts and recover from the disillusionment can be very strengthening. Can you recall how you felt after overcoming some difficult task in the past? Similarly, you and your partner will gain a great sense of strength and renewal as you break through the storm clouds and into the light of renewal. You need only a bit of a break in the clouds to know you are making progress. Some couples re-enter the romance phase with a new appreciation for each other. Others, re-enter the early commitment stage and try to re-launch the relationship.

"There is a solution to every problem and you just may not like the solution."

Some couples will be unable or choose not to seek resolution to their power struggles. They will enter a phase of **resignation**.

Those who have chosen to work at their power struggles and have re-energized their commitments may enter a **reality phase**.

Resignation Versus Reality Phase

Have you ever watched a tug-of-war competition? Each side tries to pull the other over a line marked in the sand. There is a little red flag tied to the rope as a marker. The conflict phase is much like a tug of war. Each side struggling to get the other to "see it or do it – my way". Hard work, isn't it? Why not just drop the rope and sit down together on the mark in the sand?

One party does not have to be **wrong** and the other **right**! Very little of any conflict will be resolved as long as you have these "gritted teeth and rope tugging" attitudes. One conflict will barely be resolved and another will come up. OK? Pick up your rope again and go at it! This struggle or competition to be "right" will not lead to a discovery of common goals, compromise and settlement. Solutions are hard to arrive at when both parties have closed their minds and hearts to giving and sharing.

Power Cycles

As the cycles of power struggles continue one, or perhaps both, of the partners will resign to thinking: "So this is as good as it's going to get." A sense of resignation and stagnation takes over the relationship.

Something special like a vacation or a visit from distant friends may spark a brief renewal of romance or a promise of change in the relationship. These are just flashes of energy. Real renewal will only come from openness and willingness to negotiate in love and honour and trust.

Blocking Openness

Openness can be blocked when some couples actually agree not to discuss important issues by simply not speaking about it (them) – ever! This unspoken agreement not to speak is somehow intended to avoid conflict. They live a life **around** one another. Cohabiting. Living a life of independence. Being "nice" to each other. Finding their own excitement in work, career, children, friendships, hobbies, travel, politics . . . anything but the relationship itself.

The "hush-hush" relationship allows them to live/survive and have a safe, comfortable life together. Their intimacy suffers from the blows of indifference. Emotional and sexual communication are usually greatly decreased. Any sexual encounters are less frequent, predictable and often performed in silence.

This kind of relationship is more like clamping a lid on a pot of boiling water. Something, sometime, somehow has got to give!

Wow! That's a real downer. Let's head for the exciting challenge of making a difference in your relationship!

Drop the Rope

Imagine a couple that drops the rope in the tug-of-war. They simply give up the power struggles. They sit together in the sand with a nice picnic lunch and talk things over in comfort. They live in the sense of "possibility" that life together can and will be better. Communication, negotiation, compromise, tolerance – big words, indeed. But very powerful words on the journey to a renewed relationship. Each time you resolve a conflict through dialogue and negotiation you prove a vital point. "Yes, we **can** do this!" Your individuality blossoms and you take a more personal interest in your partner.

It's something to take a risk by being open about issues. Negotiating solutions requires being honest about yourself and with others. You and your partner show your vulnerability. If this vulnerability can be accepted and respected, you are well on the way to regaining mutual acceptance and respect. Tough work! You become best friends again. Worth the effort!

Now, as best friends, there is a new equality in the relationship. Now you can build on your strengths and overcome your potentials for growth – together.

Renewed openness and vulnerability with one another releases a new energy. You feel free to inquire about and investigate your own sexuality. You can examine how you relate together as a couple. Now, in comfort, you can do something about your sexual relationship. Now you have a comfort in seeking a much deeper emotional and sexual intimacy together. Now you can make way for the **full commitment** phase of your loving relationship.

"A person is a person because of other people."
South African Truth

How Does Love Grow?

- **Falling in Love:** Like tumbling down grassy hills. Fun, exciting and not a lot of care or control. "Whee, isn't this FUN!"
- **Crawling in Love:** Slow, reluctant to change. Can't make significant commitments.
- **Leaning in Love:** Could be convinced – but maybe not. We'll see.
- **Growing in Love:** After all the tumult of falling in love. Or after starting over again. A more balanced, caring, compassionate look at being in love. Patient, thoughtful, willing to compromise, forgive, forget and let things go.
- **Learning in Love:** The phase of continuing growth in a relationship. Acknowledging mutual needs and dreams. A sharing, caring, comfortable and continuing relationship.

Full Commitment Phase

Let's talk about making choices. What kind of choices do you want to make? Do you wish to make decisions based solely on your needs without considering your partner? Conscientious choices are the result of a person's willingness to do some real soul searching. The issues and needs of each person in the relationship are openly discussed. It's time to stop avoiding and minimizing issues. Now is the time to bring them into the light.

This is a turn-around time when the act of acceptance of one another's needs, expectations and values becomes most important.

There is a rekindling of a deeper friendship. That friendship is based on a decision to care about one another – and to work hard on the relationship.

Honour and Trust

Love has matured beyond the superficial to a deep-seated sense of honour and trust. Love is a rational choice and meaningful decisions are made together. Openness and choosing will create a true partnership. A full commitment to the relationship is made.

The drizzle of disappointment ceases. That is not to say it will never rain again. Of course it will. Your love will be tested time and time again. But now you know the importance of being open and honest.

The **full commitment phase** will see a synchronization of your interests, needs and expression. Your emotional and psychological communication is closely intertwined. There is a trust that promotes a release of energy to explore new interests in your personal and sexual relationship.

The keys to the **Mature Romance Phase** are in your hands.

Mature Romance Phase

Remember the early romance phase where falling in love was described as tumbling down a grassy hill? Now, here you are in the mature romance phase where you can actually fall in love with your partner over and over again. Not a tumbling kind of love but a gentle renewal of love and devotion for each other. This was what we started looking for at the very beginning of the relationship.

But it is only through experiencing the storms in the journey of learning about each other that you are now able to enter into this phase of mature romance – and expression of love.

The power struggles, resignation and then reality have created an atmosphere where full commitment and rediscovery of romance can occur on a much deeper level.

No Ordinary Terms

As a couple, your communication with other people is based on your affection for one another. There is a bond between you that cannot be described in ordinary terms. You are equal partners. There is a deep attachment and affection for one another. And there's more! There is an excitement and creativity in your worlds of influence and responsibility.

You are still your own person. You still retain your unique personal qualities and sense of independence. Now, you and your partner have created the comfort of interdependence.

Sexual intimacy during both the full commitment and mature romance phase has moved beyond the superficial demands of "great sex". The excitement and stimulation is there but is now accompanied by an emotional depth and deep understanding. Conjugal love in the mature romance stage is experienced as two worlds joining together with mutual reverence and respect. Passion is felt as a wave of excitement and gratification rather than a momentary electrical charge of sexual stimulation.

Again, the phases of commitment and romance are like all things in nature. They come in cycles. A couple may achieve a degree of full commitment and mature romance but there will always be new experiences in the relationship. Periods of conflict and resignation will come over the horizon. You now have the experience and confidence to deal with these issues with mutual respect for each other's needs.

Love, romance and the resulting relationship are difficult to pin down to specific terms and conditions.

Couples in the full commitment and mature romance phases have experienced a renewal of their early romance through some novel event such as a second honeymoon. In some cases, it is possible for each partner to be at different phases in the cycle of relationship.

Whatever the case, your greatest assets are good will, a kind sense of humour, forgiveness and open, honest communication.

Each time you go through the phases, your skills, competency, respect and love will grow as you create your history of mutual experiences. Set your sails to the winds of change and enjoy your journey together.

"Balance is a dance you do together in life and in living."

Sexual Intimacy – Handout, see page 116.

Blended Families

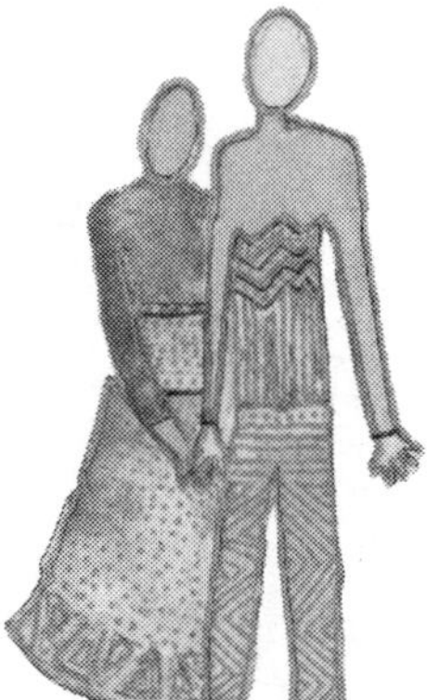

Blended Family: Mine, Yours & Ours

There have been many changes in our society in recent years. The make up of the family unit has changed dramatically. The rate of divorce has increased and with it the number of second or even third marriages for divorced individuals. **"Blended families"** is the term used when children from past marriages are brought into these new marriages.

Being involved in a previous marriage or long-term common-law relationship can provide valuable learning experience for people thinking about a new relationship. They have a fairly good idea of what they desire in a partner. They also understand some of the issues and challenges to be faced in maintaining a healthy relationship.

The blended family relationship, however, brings in a whole new series of "personal dynamics". It is more than just two adults learning how to get along. It is more than two biological parents raising their children. It is two vastly different spheres of experience and interest joined, often under duress and difficulty.

Forget the laugh track of the TV blended family sit-coms. Television is not very good at telling it like it is. The reality is: blended families require particular attention and care.

Couple Unity

"Nothing to it. We'll get married and the kids will get along just fine. We love each other and that's enough to make it all work out."

Sorry, it doesn't work that way. Entering into a blended family should not be taken lightly. There are many important issues to be considered. Dealing with them now will help avoid agony, anger and disruption later in the relationship.

Time together, for example, is a crucial element in a blended family. Life with children can be hectic. Life with two new families tends to be even more hectic as everyone deals with their new role in the relationship. That all important "time together" for couples can get lost in the pressure of doing this and that for the kids.

Take time to be together. Gulping coffee, wolfing down toast and mumbling some instructions over the breakfast table or passing along some information just before passing out from exhaustion at night just won't cut it.

What About the Children?

Good question. What about the children, indeed? Some blended family relationships have children from one or both of the families living together on a fulltime basis. Others, for example, have the children coming every other weekend. Whatever the arrangement, the needs of the children have to be given serious consideration. It is only in the wildest imaginings that we can expect everything to be "just so". Expect caution, resistance and even hostility from your spouse's children. They will not instantly fall in love with you or get along with your children. Your best efforts may not produce the immediate happy family you desire. Change takes time. Be prepared to give it a lot of time.

Here's a scenario that might occur in a modern blended family.

"Darling, please come downstairs and help me. Your kids and my kids are fighting with our kids."

Discuss Family Baggage

Everyone carries a suitcase of life experiences into the blended family. Even the youngest child has past experiences, family and friends that shape who that person is.

Every first marriage brings together family and friends from many places in our lives. The blended family introduces the added elements of non-custodial parents, anxious and perhaps competing relatives and friends.

Add visitation schedules, school issues, hockey and music lessons.

Add the importance of recognizing each child's individuality within the blended family or parts of other families.

DISCIPLINE

Discipline is defined on three levels. It is first a branch of knowledge and learning. It also can take the form of training that encourages control, character and orderliness in life. Discipline also can be strict control to enforce obedience.

All three forms of discipline are found in the blended family. It is the issue most often cited as causing difficulty or even turmoil. What may be a mild obstacle in many homes becomes a boiling cauldron of confused emotions in a blended family.

Professionals and non-professionals alike are often dismayed by the intensity of feeling generated by this issue. Family and friends are often taken aback by the amount of energy a couple gives to discussion and impassioned quarrelling over the matter of how discipline should be applied.

POWER AND CONTROL

Many couples ultimately discover that the issue is not discipline but power and control. Each member of the family is jockeying for position. The rules and boundaries are being pushed and tested.

How much and in what form should discipline be applied? And to whom? Certainly some order in any family is important. People, no matter what their age, need to know where they stand.

The couple must be unified in their loyalty to each other and the children. Parenting strategies must be agreed upon and applied with consistency. This is especially true of discipline.

The general rule of thumb for step-parents is to exercise minimal discipline until a mutual respect has been achieved. There are no rules on how long this should take. Change takes time. Family members, to the best of their ability, should be encouraged to respect each other's needs and help the adjustments go smoothly.

This early effort at "paving the way" will build a firm foundation as the family develops into a loving and respectful unit. That is the goal of discipline. Use it, not as a hammer to beat things into shape, but as a learning and training tool to mould the family unit.

Twin Goals

The twin goals of discipline are referred to in terms of "nurture" and "control".

(*Strengthening Your Step Family*, by Linda Albert and Elisabeth Einstein, American Guidance Service, Circle Pines, MN 55014-1796, 1986)

The traditional nuclear family sees the parents giving great emphasis to the "nurturing" side of discipline for their infant children. The infants are cuddled, fussed over, stroked, sung to and rocked to sleep. Practically every need of the infant child is fulfilled. The need to say "No" to the child does not exist. There is no need to limit or control the child's behaviour at this stage. Thus, a strong, loving bond is developed with each parent and the infant.

This time spent together is important to the new parents. They have plenty of time to talk things over and share ideas on how to proceed with the "control" side of discipline. The need to say "No" comes along gradually as the child develops. The parents have time to decide how they will deal with each situation as it comes along.

In this way, there is a good chance that the biological parents can develop a mutually agreeable and consistent style of parenting.

No Luxury of Time

In contrast, step-families do not enjoy this luxury of time to discover and employ the process of nurture and control discipline.

People are often thrust together, sometimes against their wishes.

"You'll just have to learn to get along" is a pat answer to a child's fears and upset. This form of discipline can create a power and control issue and take on fearful dimensions in the parent-child relationship.

Step Family Roles

Each individual in the family is just that – an individual. Children, natural parents and step-parents all have unique strengths and ideals. Each also has their own difficulties. All of these differences come forward within a blended family situation.

The Step-Parent Roles

Step-parents are advised to avoid these pitfalls:

- Trying to "replace" the child's parent. This creates loyalty conflicts for the child.
- Demanding acceptance and "instant love" from the step-child. Change in terms of progress takes time. You, like everyone else, will have to earn love and respect.
- Insisting that feelings for the step-children and the biological children are the same. They are not.
- Trying to make up for the children's parental loss by pampering and indulging the step-children.
- Insisting on family unity and sameness thus rejecting the diversity of the step-children's family background.

Effective traits for step-parents are identified in the booklet "*Pitfalls and Possibilities*" by Linda Albert and Elizabeth Einstein, New York and Tampa, Florida, 1983.

This booklet indicates that an effective step-parent would do the following:

- Recognize the importance of the non-custodial parent and the child's life background.
- Demonstrate respect for the step-child by allowing a nurturing relationship between non-custodial parents.
- Encourage visits, phone calls, gifts and letters.
- Allow the child to display photos and mementos of the biological parent.
- Acknowledge the existing bond between the new spouse and his/her children. Acknowledge that it is natural to feel closer to one's biological children. This acknowledgement reduces jealousy and competition for time and attention. It controls resentment when children and their natural parent need to be alone.

- Allow time for relationships to develop as they accept and respect new family forms and dimensions.
- Accept that perfection is impossible; understand that family life will not always be happy; accept that problems are a reality of life and living.
- Permit the children to belong to two families without constantly harping on the matter or referring to it in conversation.
- Allow the children to spend time with peers, the other parent and at outside activities without fearing that the stability of the step-family is threatened.
- Use time away from the children to enhance the relationship with his/her spouse.

The Natural Parent

The process of adjustment for all concerned creates some degree of anxiety. This is particularly so for the natural parent within the blended family. The natural parents are often described as the hub of the wheel. They spend a considerable amount of time just keeping peace between their natural child and the step-parent. It is good that the step-parent be allowed to deal effectively with the child. It is also good that the natural parent continues to offer support and encouragement to the step-parent in this relationship with the natural children.

The Children and Step-Children

Somehow children have been disenfranchised in society. They are presumed to be unable to speak for themselves, offer a valid opinion or have feelings worthy of consideration. As a result BIG people take over their lives and make all kinds of decisions without even consulting them.

Separation, divorce and remarriage are traumatic events. Children do not watch idly from the sidelines as they would at a sports competition. They and their feelings are deeply, deeply immersed in the turmoil, upset and anger.

Parents need to exercise the three C's of love – care, caution and courtesy – as everyone tumbles through changes in relationships. Be sensitive to the number of changes that have occurred and are still occurring. There is a sense of lack of control that the child experiences as a result of the changes.

Fear of the unknown, frustration, sorrow and anger are natural reactions for anyone who has had his or her life turned upside down. Why would this not be so for children? Acting out towards their parent/step-parent and step-brothers and sisters is common. These reactions are symptoms of a child who has been hurt and is still grieving the loss of the original family.

Above all things, these children need a kind, gentle and understanding love. Care, sensitivity to their needs and patience will help them over the difficulties of change.

Support Groups and Counselling

Parents should not hesitate to search out blended family educational support groups or family counselling. These services will help all members of the blended family deal with the inevitable differences they will encounter as they build their family relationship.

Exercise

Recognizing Family Changes

Change is a fact of life. The bringing together of a blended family will create many changes. Some for the better. Some for the worse. The true measure of success in change is to find some indication of **progress**.

The following exercise is designed so that each member of the blended family will be able to identify positive (progressive) and negative changes.

Step One: Complete the questionnaire.

Question #1: What are the changes that have occurred as a result of the blended family?

Question #2: What changes are for the better?

Question #3: What changes are for the worse?

Step Two: Explain why each change is for the better or for the worse.

Step Three: Discuss your responses with your fiance (partner or spouse)and the children.

Financial Considerations

Whose Money Is It?

Who earns how much money? Who spends how much money? How much is "my" money, "your" money and "our" money?

These questions are the foundation for one of the most common issues that adversely affect couples. How do we agree on how much to spend, where to spend it or when to save and invest?

"Whose Money Is It" is designed to encourage you and your partner to take a serious look at your spending and saving habits, plus the attitudes and desires around how you spend your hard-earned money.

Misunderstandings, disagreements or one partner imposing his or her views on the other can result from each partner's different feelings or views about how money should be spent. Quarrels over money, like quarrels over many other things, may be more about a difference in values or about a loss of control.

Rather than facing the money issue, many individuals choose to put on the dark glasses and operate on their own. This can leave their partners with a sense of being alienated, confused or suspicious of the other's motives.

Fill in the Blanks: Do You Recognize a Situation Like This?

"____________just sort of fudges around whenever I ask about things like salaries, savings and investments. How can we plan a life together if I don't know how much money is coming in?"

"_________ will go out and buy stuff on a whim – just spend a couple of hundred bucks on the darndest junk. We hardly ever have enough to pay the bills. I really wonder if _______ knows how much this upsets me?"

It is important that couples come to a mutually agreeable arrangement about budgeting and spending priorities. Taking the time to discuss "money matters" and then working together in mutual trust will help create a healthier and less-worrisome relationship.

Bumper Sticker Snicker:

"I Shop Like A Bull. I CHARGE Everything!"

Share and Share Alike

Individuals within a marriage relationship must be aware that liability is shared between both partners on loans or acquisitions that were purchased under the action of joint ownership and verified by both partners' signatures. This includes joint credit cards, bank accounts, joint ownership of a home, car, major appliances and recreation equipment.

Generally, spouses are not liable for debts incurred by their spouse on loans, acquisitions and purchases that were not bought under a joint ownership agreement. If your signature was not on the legal forms related to the purchase or loan you are not necessarily liable.

Words of Wisdom From a Bankruptcy Trustee

There are many financial institutions that offer financial counselling to individuals and couples. Helen Czinkota, representing Deloitte and Touche in Regina, Saskatchewan, counsels people on bankruptcy and feels that too many couples fall into the trap of financial woes because they do not pay enough attention to their spending habits. Helen feels that it is imperative that couples work together to create a household budget.

The creation of a budget also helps to create general rules on spending family income.

Example of a "rule": We agree not to make a purchase of over $100.00 without consulting each other.

Helen's experience, along with that of thousands of other financial counsellors, simply reinforces the need for couples to talk, declare, consult and, in its simplest terms, spend less than they make.

Today's consumers are coming to realize that they must learn to stop spending and start saving. Interest payments on loans, including credit cards, for example, have become a large part of the household budget.

Many families are caught in the grind of living from pay cheque to pay cheque. High, dual-income earners as well as low-income earners find themselves in a worrisome state that can suck the energy from a relationship and lifestyle.

Evaluating your situation and setting limits and realistic goals can ease the burden and give you a sense of confidence.

Taking Responsibility for Managing the Money

The roadside of life is littered with people who have given up the responsibility for looking after the money to their partner. Perhaps they were forced into this situation or just "weren't interested".

The classic result of this is the spouse (often the wife) who is unable to perform even the simplest financial transaction should the partner leave due to separation or divorce or death.

Those with uncontrollable spending habits (or compulsive gamblers) appreciate this environment as do those who are very controlling in nature. As pointed out before, this arrangement does not lead to a healthy, trusting relationship. Awareness around where the money is coming from and where it is going is crucial. One solution is to have one spouse monitor where the money is being spent within and outside the home. The other partner could take on the responsibility of reconciling the bank books so as to be aware of the cash flow and balances.

How Can We Save Money? Let Us Count the Ways

Financial "Whoas" Can Stop Financial Woes

It may appear simplistic at first but the best way to save money is to **spend less than you bring in.** That may require some adjustment in thinking. You will have to decide if you really **need** that item or if you are just falling into the old buying pattern of having more "stuff".

Keep in mind that it is the job of the advertisers, stores and sales people to convince you that your life is not complete without their "New – Improved" item. You make choices based on your values. Decide for yourself and as a couple what really matters. You will then be amazed at how you can chop, slash and burn your way through old spending habits.

Short-Term and Long-Term Goals

"If you don't know where you are going, how will you know when you get there?"

It is important for couples to make short- and long-term financial goals that are realistic and **mutually** agreed upon. Write the goals down and review them on a semi-annual basis.

Short-term goals may include car purchase, repairs, big ticket household items and maintenance – and a vacation.

Long-term goals may include buying a house, investments, retirement savings and insurance contributions.

Tips on Picking a Financial Planner

Financial planning is one of the major growth industries in Canada. Their advertising is in all the media. Financial planners are often equipped to sell insurance, retirement funds, education plans for children and can offer guidance on loan acquisitions and loan repayments.

As in any purchase, you are advised to be prepared and ask a lot of questions. Shop around. Take your time. Do not make any commitment of **your** money until you and your spouse are confident in the experience and knowledge of your financial planner.

Where There's a Will . . .

Do you and your spouse have legal wills? Incredibly, it is estimated that over 75 percent of Canadians to not have written wills.

What does this have to do with financial planning? Lots! If you or your spouse dies without a will, the courts will take over and determine how your estate is dispersed. It's better to have a will, to ensure that these very important financial matters are looked after – the way **you** want, rather than have the courts decide for you after your death.

Basic Budget Equations

No Budget Plan = anxiety, worry, arguments, hurt feelings, loss of sleep, loss of self respect when bills are not paid, humiliation when the bank calls, embarrassment when creditors and bill collectors pressure for payment.

Commitment to Budget Plan = peace of mind, control, fewer arguments, financial contentment, ability to plan ahead, no fear of answering the phone.

It's your choice!

General Guideline for Family Spending

Note: ***Every family situation is different. The following percentages are guidelines to help you identify your budget basics.***

Shelter – (including mortgage payment and interest – or rent)	30%
Food – (including groceries and items such as soaps, tissue, etc., not appliances, etc. – purchased at grocery stores)	30%
Transportation – fuel, maintenance, vehicle registrations, bus fares	10%
Clothing	8%
Savings, Investments, RRSP's	5%
Insurance (vehicle, life, disability, household)	4%
Household Repairs (including garage and fence)	5%
Health Care	4%
Recreation	4%

Stop the Budget Leaks

Many financial consultants urge their clients to record **every** purchase they make over a period of six weeks. This will provide an excellent answer to the question "Where on earth does all the money go?"

Be brutally honest. Write down everything – a pack of gum, parking meter fees, $5.00 here, $2.00 there. Be sure to include credit card and other interest charges.

Now you know where the money goes.

"A sale price is no bargain if you buy something you don't really need."
Mike Grenby, Financial Adviser

A Budget is a Road Map

A written budget will guide you down the road to successful money management. Plan to review your budget periodically. If you are not living together at this time, simply use estimated figures.

Setting Up Our Monthly Budget

1. Expenses

Monthly Expenses (Fixed)		Monthly Expenses (Flexible)	Planned	Spent
Mortgage or Rent	$______		Planned	Spent
Utilities		**Food**	$ ______	$ ______
Gas	______		______	______
Power	______	**Clothing**	______	______
Water	______		______	______
Telephone	______	**Transportation** (car, gas, oil, public transport, parking)	______ ______ ______ ______	______ ______ ______ ______
Cable T.V.	______	**Entertainment**	______	______
Savings	______	**Household** (paper products, minor repairs, light bulbs, laundromat, etc.)	______ ______ ______ ______	______ ______ ______ ______
Insurance		**Education** (school supplies, tuition)	______ ______	______ ______
Home	______	**Health** (medical, dental drugs)	______ ______	______ ______
Life	______	**Gifts**		
Car	______	(Christmas)	______	______
Medical	______	(Other)	______	______
Other	______	**Donations**		
Taxes	______	(Church)	______	______
Credit Card Interest	______	(Charities)	______	______
Fixed Debts (identify: car loan bank loan)	______ ______ ______ ______	**Alcohol**	______	______
Child Care	______	**Tobacco**	______	______
Alimony/Child Support	______	**Personal**	______	______
		Miscellaneous	______	______
Total Fixed Expenses	$______	**Total Flexible Expenses**	$ ______	$ ______
		+		
		Total Fixed Expenses	$ ______	$ ______
		=		
		Total Monthly Expenses	$ ______	$ ______

Monthly Net Income (from page 90) minus Total Monthly Expenses = Balance

$ ______________ – $ ______________ = $ ______________

2. Income

Monthly Income		Irregular Income	
Net employment income $	______	(estimate amount per year)	
Spouse's net employment income	______	GST rebate	______
Investment income	______	Maturing CSBs	______
Pension income	______	Investment income	______
Annuity income	______	Tax refund	______
RRIF income	______	Other income	______
Maintenance/ support income	______		
EI/Disability income	______		
Child benefit income	______		
Other monthly income	______		
TOTAL MONTHLY INCOME $	______	TOTAL ANNUAL IRREGULAR INCOME $	______

TOTAL MONTHLY INCOME $ ______

TOTAL MONTHLY EXPENSES $ ______

BALANCE: SURPLUS OR (SHORTAGE) $ ______

If there is a SHORTAGE between monthly income and monthly cost of living:

Are there realistic ways to increase income? How? ______

Are there realistic ways to decrease expenses? How? ______

If there is a SURPLUS of income after monthly cost of living:

Will you use this as your "payment ability" for debts? ______

Will you save or invest this for your financial goals? ______

Take Charge of Your Money!

- Learn some Latin. "Caveat Emptor" means – "Let The Buyer Beware"!
- Consider the advertiser as a potential threat. Be wary of the sales pitch on something you don't need. Separate your "wants" from your "needs".
- Recognize that sales people are, by and large, honest, hard-working people who, like you, have to make a living. They want you to decide NOW so they can close the sale. Do not be pressured or swayed. Take your time.
- Shop around and then "mull over" any major purchase for a day or two. You may decide not to buy – or make a different choice.
- Consult with your spouse regarding any significant purchases. Set limits on how much you will spend.
- Don't buy it unless you have the cash. This will greatly reduce impulse buying.
- Avoid buying something just because it is "On Sale". Everything is "On Sale".
- Writing a cheque when you know your account can't cover it is dishonest and will cost you hefty N.S.F. charges. It can also affect your credit record and personal reputation.
- Do you really need two cars? A riding lawnmower?
- Do basic home maintenance yourself – or barter your skills with another person.
- Find a good car mechanic, plumber, electrician and other service providers **before you need one**.
- Do as many errands as possible in one trip.
- Take care of your body and mind to avoid serious illness. Proper diet, exercise and a good mental attitude will help keep you healthy.
- Move to less expensive accommodation.
- Cancel all those magazines. Use the library services instead.
- Do not shop for groceries when you are hungry.
- Buy generic foods, drugs and home products. Make a list of what you need and stick to it.

There are many more creative ways to save! Brainstorm with your spouse and family and see how many more you can come up with.

New! Improved!

Exciting Ways To Get Rid Of Your Money!

- Spending gobs of money on lotteries, VLTs and bingo.
- Buying a new car which will then depreciate about 25% when you drive it off the lot.
- Restaurant meals – OK once in a while as a treat but these can make a real dent in your dollar.
- Life insurance policies for your children.
- Boats and other water toys. Rent one when you want one.
- Carrying a wad of credit cards, thus ending up in the jungle of debt payments and heavy interest charges.
- Paying one credit card by debiting another.
- Lavishing expensive or "guilt" gifts on family, friends, or yourself. Hugs and little remembrances are fondly received.
- Lending money to family and friends without promissory notes.
- Designer-label clothing.
- Low-interest saving accounts. Take an interest in your money and be prepared to move it around.
- Buying into any deal or promotion that is "**Too Good To Be True**". It usually is – too good to be true.
- TV shopping, TV offers, telephone solicitors requiring that you decide to buy or order "right now".
- Buying anything that is **New and Improved!**
- Buying **anything** just because someone else has it.
- Breaking your commitment to stick to your budget.

Where Does the Money Go?

Joan enjoys eating in restaurants with her family and friends. It's convenient, no dishes to do and – it's fun!

If Joan goes to a restaurant on the average of three times per week and orders food ranging from a Big Snack to a full-course meal, she will spend:

$30.00 per week

$120.00 per month

$1440.00 per year.

Plus around $200.00 for Tips!

If Joan were to have her friends over for shared suppers and treat herself to dinner out once a week she would save enough money to take a nice little vacation.

Larry smokes an average of a pack a day. Larry is investing in his health and wellness to the tune of:

$6.00 per day

$42.00 per week

$168.00 per month

$2,016 per year.

If Larry saved even five dollars a day rather than buying smokes, he would have a nice little nest egg put away.

It's your money!

It's your choice!

"That's Life"

Humour Helps!

Yes, my friend, humour – and laughter – help! They are good medicine – not necessarily the best medicine. Other elements of personal "best medicine" are a strong affirmation of your own self-worth, the ability to get along with yourself and others and a personal balance of wellness.

That said, helpful humour and healthy laughter are indeed great assets to our daily life. Be sure to take your medicine every day.

Humour and laughter are contagious.

They are part of a solo performance where you can learn to laugh **at** yourself. That is, not take yourself so seriously. You will soon be able to spread this feeling around in your dealings with others.

Healthy humour and laughter let people gather in trust and honour and share the invigoration and joy of being together. In this manner we can laugh **with** each other.

Humour and laughter are good body medicine too.

Research indicates that laughter creates a natural body chemical called endorphins. It's the stuff that gives you that "feel good" feeling when you laugh.

Laughter also causes us to breath deeper thus oxygenating our cardiovascular system. Simply stated – we breath more, get more oxygen to the body parts – and we feel better.

A good belly laugh gives us an organ massage too. And the eyes sparkle. And sometimes we laugh – until we cry. And that's good too!

Laughter is also great soul medicine.

We can forget all our cares and woes (whoas, if you prefer) for a while when we laugh. So you see, it's really good to make use of our natural sense of humour and **learn to laugh!**

Learn to LAUGH? Yes, some of us have to learn to laugh. So much of our culture is bent on suppressing this most wonderful and holy of our natural gifts and resources. To some, laughing means not being in control. It is considered improper, unprofessional, undignified and a sign of immaturity.

Phooey! Good, kind, supportive and appropriate humour – and the smiles and laughter it generates, is at home in any place.

Why not give it a try – **just for laughs?**

The Impact of Attitude

You ARE your attitude. No one else can decide your attitude for you. A positive, optimistic attitude is essential for success in business, sports and personal wellness. The attitude you bring into your relationship will also play a big part in whether or not it is a success.

There are many important benefits in demonstrating a positive, supportive attitude in your marriage relationship.

A positive attitude lets you feel good about yourself and others. You are more energetic and display greater enthusiasm for life. A positive attitude encourages a spirit of team work where both partners contribute in important and significant ways.

A positive attitude allows you to be approachable and communicate effectively. You can experience greater satisfaction in your relationship, make the most of good and bad situations and deal more effectively with stress.

You'll be better able to focus on what is really important in your relationship and create balance as you are more open to new ideas.

A positive attitude will help carry you through difficult times.

Eight Ways to an Enthusiastic Attitude

1. Say something positive to every person you meet every day (including yourself).
2. See something positive in every situation. (A man with a bald spot is the first to know it's raining.)
3. Make a habit of thinking and living in "the possibility" that something good will happen.
4. Learn to ask yourself, "Why Not?"
5. Do it now. Describe "it".
6. Always expect the best.
7. Count your blessings, not your troubles.
8. Become a positive reactionary. It's your choice.

"Whether you think you CAN or think you CAN'T, in either case, you are absolutely right"

You attitude is YOUR CHOICE! *"IF IT IS TO BE IT IS UP TO ME"*

Bridging Stress With Success

- Not all stress is bad. There are many symptoms of stress. Investigate the source or core of your feelings – and the thoughts and ideas that you associate with them.
- Your are your ATTITUDE. Positive and supportive SELF TALK will help you through difficult situations. Encourage yourself. You are a good and valuable person. Don't let anyone tell you otherwise, including yourself!
- Take care of your whole body. Even the parts you can't see need lots of TLC (heart, lungs, muscles, brain and veins). They are your "body buddies". Energize them with exercise and fresh air.
- You are what you eat! Eat regular well-balanced meals. Reduce fat – increase fibre. Ease off the booze, drugs, caffeine and junk.
- Relax. Learn relaxation techniques to unwind physically and mentally. Use imagery to imagine or see relaxing places or things. Meditation lets you concentrate on spiritual or gentle thoughts.
- Get rid of the Perfection Demon. Comparing yourself to others can be destructive. Do the best you can with what you've got.
- Uncomplicate. Set realistic goals, establish priorities. As you would clean out your garage or basement, clean out your personal priorities list. A lot of "stuff" just doesn't matter.
- Avoid dwelling on the negatives. How many past worries came true? Worry takes a lot of physical and mental energy. Concern yourself with what you can change. Read the Serenity Prayer, page 102.
- Change. Take small steps. It's like building a campfire. Be patient. It will take time. Rapid change can create more distress.
- You deserve a break! Add variety and sparkle. Listen to children laugh. Watch the wind. Find a special place to be by yourself. Reward yourself. Take time to enjoy living.
- Give away whatever you need. Forgiveness, kindness, joy, love, encouragement. These are just a few of your renewable natural resources. The more you give away – the more you will get! True!
- There are lots of great books, tapes and support groups that deal with personal well-being. Ask for help. Talk things over with someone you trust. Read more. Writing a journal is very helpful. Write whenever the spirit moves you.

Life is a journey. Living is an art, not a science.

Every day's a good day. Some are better than others.

The "Take a Break – Take a Breath" Stress Breaker

Situations:

Somebody is in your face about something and your are beginning to boil . . . **or** –

You remember an upsetting incident or what somebody said in the past . . . **or** –

You are all angst about something you think someone will do or say in the future. (Wow! You are a Swami, too!) . . . **or** –

You are working hard at something and it is just not going the way you want . . . All thumbs . . . A few cuss words . . . **or** –

Some goof cuts you off in traffic . . . "You blinkity blank!"

Reactions: Frustration, anger, annoyance, pain or upset in the gut. Increased heart rate, tension . . . and more!

Action: retaliate, yell, swear, burn, drive faster, get upset, blow horn, finger salute . . .

WHOA! Hold your horses – and your breath!

Step Out of the Circle. Take a Break. Take a Breath.

- Simply take IN a "DEEP as you can BREATH" through your nose. Do this slowly, or you'll rip something important.
- Hold this breath for a couple of seconds so your lungs can use up some of the oxygen. You should feel some sensation in your "gut".
- Then – let your breath go – slowly – through pursed lips. Like you are whistling. Go ahead and whistle – but only one note.
- Do this 3 – 4 – 10 times as time permits. Or as required to ease the tension.

It works!

Ten Commandments of Human Relations!

1. SPEAK TO PEOPLE and yourself in gentle terms – there is nothing nicer than a cheerful word of greeting.
2. SMILE. Frowning is hard work. It takes 72 muscles to frown and only 14 to smile.
3. CALL PEOPLE BY THEIR NAME. The sound of one's own name is sweet music to the ears.
4. BE FRIENDLY AND HELPFUL. If you would like to have friends, be a friend.
5. BE CORDIAL. Speak and act in a sense of pleasure and enjoyment.
6. BE GENUINELY INTERESTED IN OTHERS. There is something about everyone that you can like – if you really try.
7. BE GENEROUS WITH PRAISE. Praise is like encouragement. Be cautious with criticism.
8. BE CONSIDERATE. Your feelings and the feelings of others are worthy of respect. There are usually three points of view. Yours, the other person's and a compromise.
9. BE WILLING TO SERVE. Give the gifts you have been given.
10. ADD GENEROUS HELPINGS OF healthy humour, patience and humility.

Happiness is nothing more than health and a poor memory.

Albert Schweitzer

Slow Abdominal Breathing

This technique uses slow deep breaths.

- Place your hands on your abdomen (stomach) and breathe in deeply. Your hands should rise. As you breathe out your hands should fall. (Some suggest the body centre is located just below the navel [belly button]. Found it?)
- As you breathe in you can count to yourself "In, one two" and as you breathe out you can count "Out, one two." With each breath out you will feel yourself becoming more and more relaxed.

Breathe in and out slowly.

Present Moment Breathing

This technique requires a focus on an object, a sensation or a phrase.

A simple meditation is the focus on the breath as it enters and leaves the nostrils.

"Allow the body to just breathe naturally and bring the attention to the breath contact as it enters the nostrils. Bring the awareness to the sense of touch of the air as it passes in and passes out . . . keep your attention at one precise point and note the sensation that accompanies each breath as it flows in and out of the body in the natural breathing process.

If the attention strays, bring it back to the touching point that notices the breath as it comes and goes at the nostrils . . . sensations arise in the body."

Thoughts arise in the mind. They come and go like bubbles.
(Stephen Levine, A *Gradual Awakening*)

SERENITY PRAYER

(from Alcoholics Anonymous)

God grant me the serenity to accept the things I cannot change

The courage to change the things I can

And the wisdom to know the difference

Exercises -

Marriage & Relationships

The Following Pages are Exercises that will Help Couples Explore and Define Their Expectations and Attitudes on:

- Spirituality
- Sexual Intimacy
- Family Backgrounds, Values and Expectations
- Good Communication and Nurturing Your Relationship

These pages are perforated so they can be easily removed and photocopied. You can do these exercises separately or together. You can discuss them and learn to communicate more openly with one another. By keeping the originals, and recopying them, and redoing these exercises, you will be able to explore the growth and changes in your attitudes and relationship.

Christian Marriage

Exercise #1

Complete the following sentences. Exchange these with your partner and discuss them.

1. To me, God is ______________________________

____

2. I felt closest to God when ______________________________

____

3. I know God is close to us as a couple when ______________________________

____

4. I have trouble accepting these teachings of my church ______________________________

____

5. I live out my belief by ______________________________

____

6. My favourite spiritual practice is ______________________________

____

7. I think it's important for us as a couple to ______________________________

____

Christian Marriage

Exercise #2

Complete the following rating scales by choosing a number that best represents how you feel about the issues presented. Exchange these with your partner and discuss them after carefully reading each other's responses.

Rate your judgement of the following:

1. I am freely committing myself in this marriage.

1	2	3	4	5
Not sure at all		I have some uncertainty		Absolutely sure

2. I am free of anyone's demands, fears, pressures or threats in making this commitment.

1	2	3	4	5
Not sure at all		I have some uncertainty		Absolutely sure

3. I believe my spouse will see me and treat me as an equal.

1	2	3	4	5
Not sure at all		I have some uncertainty		Absolutely sure

4. I believe that faith will help to protect and nurture a healthy marriage.

1	2	3	4	5
Not sure at all		I have some uncertainty		Absolutely sure

5. I want to remain open to change for my own personal growth and my behaviour with others.

1	2	3	4	5
Not sure at all		I have some uncertainty		Absolutely sure

6. I want to learn to listen to my spouse's needs and ideas.

1	2	3	4	5
Not sure at all		I have some uncertainty		Absolutely sure

7. I want to learn to speak of my needs, feelings and ideas to my spouse openly and frequently.

1	2	3	4	5
Not sure at all		I have some uncertainty		Absolutely sure

8. I want our marriage to be a faith-filled Christian marriage.

1	2	3	4	5
Not sure at all		I have some uncertainty		Absolutely sure

Christian Marriage

Exercise #3

How do you want to live out your faith in your marriage? Take the following list and prioritize the items from the most to the least important to you. Exchange lists and attempt to develop a joint plan for your marriage.

1. Personal prayer
2. Personal scripture study
3. Shared prayer with spouse and others
4. Going to church regularly
5. Studying about one's church and one's faith
6. Exploring issues of social justice and the needs of the poor and the oppressed
7. Volunteer work on church committees and programs
8. Volunteer work in the community at large to serve the needs of others
9. Praying at meal times and at the beginning or end of the day
10. Giving money to one's church
11. Giving money to organizations working for the poor
12. Celebrating special Christian feast days such as Christmas, Easter, Pentecost with family attendance at church and having a family meal together
13. Preparing one's own children and others to be members of the church

Sexual Intimacy

Exercise #1

Expectations and Attitudes Checklist

Rate on the following scale how strongly you feel or believe the following:

1. I am comfortable with my own body.

1	2	3	4	5
Strongly Disagree				Strongly Agree

2. I feel comfortable looking at or touching my own body.

1	2	3	4	5
Strongly Disagree				Strongly Agree

3. I feel positive about my male or femaleness.

1	2	3	4	5
Strongly Disagree				Strongly Agree

4. Women are more interested in romance than sexual pleasure.

1	2	3	4	5
Strongly Disagree				Strongly Agree

5. Men are more interested in sexual pleasure than in romance.

1	2	3	4	5
Strongly Disagree				Strongly Agree

6. I believe passion is the most important ingredient for really enjoying sexual intimacy.

1	2	3	4	5
Strongly Disagree				Strongly Agree

7. I believe romance is the most important ingredient for really enjoying sexual intimacy.

1	2	3	4	5
Strongly Disagree				Strongly Agree

8. I believe open, affectionate and responsive communication with one another are the most important ingredients for really enjoying sexual intimacy.

1	2	3	4	5
Strongly Disagree				Strongly Agree

9. For sexual intimacy to be really enjoyable, it must be spontaneous.

1	2	3	4	5
Strongly Disagree				Strongly Agree

10. Men need sexual pleasure more than do women.

1	2	3	4	5
Strongly Disagree				Strongly Agree

11. I expect almost every act of conjugal love to be special.

1	2	3	4	5
Strongly Disagree				Strongly Agree

12. I expect almost every act of conjugal love to lead to a physical/emotional climax.

1	2	3	4	5
Strongly Disagree				Strongly Agree

13. I believe it's okay to give in to my mate's demands for lovemaking even when I'm not too interested.

1	2	3	4	5
Strongly Disagree				Strongly Agree

14. I believe it's okay to say no to my mate's sexual advances.

1	2	3	4	5
Strongly Disagree				Strongly Agree

15. I expect my mate to respect my decision not to make love at times when I don't want to.

1	2	3	4	5
Strongly Disagree				Strongly Agree

16. I would rate my drive for sexual pleasure as:

1	2	3	4	5
LOW (at least monthly)		MEDIUM (at least or almost weekly)		HIGH (almost daily)

17. I think it would be exciting to make love in places other than the bedroom.

1	2	3	4	5
Strongly Disagree				Strongly Agree

18. I expect my mate to respect my requests to stop something during our lovemaking if it hurt or made me feel uncomfortable in some way.

1	2	3	4	5
Strongly Disagree				Strongly Agree

19. I believe women enjoy men who are domineering and more aggressive in lovemaking.

1	2	3	4	5
Strongly Disagree				Strongly Agree

20. I believe men enjoy women who are more passive and compliant in lovemaking.

1	2	3	4	5
Strongly Disagree				Strongly Agree

21. I believe we should take turns setting the stage and initiating lovemaking.

1	2	3	4	5
Strongly Disagree				Strongly Agree

22. Personal cleanliness is important to me for wanting to make love with my mate.

1	2	3	4	5
Strongly Disagree				Strongly Agree

23. I expect to talk about, confront and negotiate about our lovemaking.

1	2	3	4	5
Strongly Disagree				Strongly Agree

24. I expect my mate to be sexually faithful throughout marriage.

1	2	3	4	5
Strongly Disagree				Strongly Agree

25. I expect myself to be sexually faithful throughout our marriage.

1	2	3	4	5
Strongly Disagree				Strongly Agree

26. I believe it would be too hard for me to forgive my mate for adultery.

1	2	3	4	5
Strongly Disagree				Strongly Agree

27. Adultery is not a sufficient reason for ending a marriage.

1	2	3	4	5
Strongly Disagree				Strongly Agree

28. I believe affection and a good mood are a necessary prerequisite for lovemaking.

1	2	3	4	5
Strongly Disagree				Strongly Agree

29. I believe making love will be a good way of getting over a bad day together.

1	2	3	4	5
Strongly Disagree				Strongly Agree

30. A healthy friendship together will go a long way to keep our sexual relationship exciting.

1	2	3	4	5
Strongly Disagree				Strongly Agree

31. Sexual pleasure is a good reward for getting something you wanted.

1	2	3	4	5
Strongly Disagree				Strongly Agree

32. I would be excited by my mate using sexually vulgar language while we initiate lovemaking.

1	2	3	4	5
Strongly Disagree				Strongly Agree

33. I believe making love would be a good way of getting over being hurt or angry about something my spouse said or did.

1	2	3	4	5
Strongly Disagree				Strongly Agree

34. I believe it is possible for a husband to sexually abuse his wife and that this is totally unacceptable to me.

1	2	3	4	5
Strongly Disagree				Strongly Agree

35. I believe I need _________ foreplay to really enjoy myself when making love.

Medium	Some	A lot

36. I believe that making love is a sufficient way of letting my spouse know I love him/her.

1	2	3	4	5
Strongly Disagree				Strongly Agree

37. I believe we are equally responsible for our fertility, sexual intimacy, pregnancy and family planning.

1	2	3	4	5
Strongly Disagree				Strongly Agree

38. I believe we have a clear understanding of one another about our values and expectations for responsible sexual intimacy and family planning.

1	2	3	4	5
Strongly Disagree				Strongly Agree

39. Telling me how beautiful I am, how much you love me, how much you enjoy me would be exciting and fulfilling during our conjugal loving.

1	2	3	4	5
Strongly Disagree				Strongly Agree

40. I believe I will be more receptive to making love when we are close, affectionate, and getting along than when we are angry, frustrated, withdrawn or disappointed with one another.

1	2	3	4	5
Strongly Disagree				Strongly Agree

41. I will be ________ hurt if you push me away or turn away from me when I make sexual advances to you.

Greatly	Somewhat Hurt	Rarely Hurt

42. For me, hugging, kissing, holding one another, touching one another and talking quietly together is _________ genital activity.

More Important Than	Just as Important As	Not as Important As

43. I am worried that I will not meet your needs or expectations sexually.

1	2	3	4	5
Strongly Disagree				Strongly Agree

Sexual Intimacy

Exercise #2

Choose two questions from the Expectations and Attitudes Checklist that are the most important to you and ask your partner about them. "What I really want to know from you is how you feel about this . . . "

Sexual Intimacy

Exercise #3

1. Exchange your Expectations and Attitudes Checklist and go through the questions, trying to listen to the other's feelings and understanding about each item. Ask questions but do not make any opinionated or judgemental comments about your partner's responses. Your goal is to listen to one another and try to understand your similarities and differences.

2. A few days later, identify one or two issues from the Expectations and Attitudes Checklist where you differed significantly from one another and which you believe could be a source of misunderstanding or conflict.

Try to explore these issues with one another in an open, respectful conversation.

Sexual Intimacy

Handout

What ruins a good long-term sexual relationship?

1. Selfish gimmicks and obsessions such as porn movies and books, aggressiveness, acting out fantasy, vulgar talk, pressuring the other to do certain acts.

2. Pain, fatigue, anxiety, depression and fear.

3. Verbal abuse – name calling, belittling, condemnation, viciousness.

4. Loss of trust, and loss of respect for one's spouse due to physical threat, infidelity and/or mind games (emotional blackmail, jealousy, guilt tripping, mind reading, lying, power tripping).

5. Avoidance of one's spouse, ignoring the communication of one's spouse, excessive silence and emotional withdrawal.

What enhances a good long-term sexual relationship?

1. Kindness, gentleness, goodness, forgiveness, acceptance, patience, faithfulness and self-control. These qualities must be visible in actions and words with one another.

2. Good communication skills and habits usually lead to better sexual intimacy, while poor communication skills and habits almost always lead to diminished sexual intimacy.

Family Backgrounds, Values and Expectations

Exercise #1

Take a moment now to reflect on your Family of Origin.

In your family of origin, how did your mom and dad:

1. Express anger
2. Show affection
3. Divide up domestic roles and responsibilities
4. Handle money matters
5. Deal with crises
6. Divide up parenting roles and responsibilities
7. Handle employment demands from each other
8. Handle pet beefs or demands from each other

Do you agree or disagree with the way your parents handled these issues?

Who are you most like in your responsiveness to these issues?

How?

Family Backgrounds, Values and Expectations

Exercise #2

Values and Priorities Checklist

Go through the list of values listed and choose the fifteen which are most important to you. Prioritize them from the least to the most important (1 would be the most important and 15 the least important). List any others that you feel would need to be included. Compare your list with one another. Are there differences in kind or differences in priority?

1. ***Loyalty*** – Maintaining important connections and commitments to others
2. ***Power*** – Having authority and influence
3. ***Independence*** – Having freedom of thought and action
4. ***Education*** – Continued growth in knowledge and skills
5. ***Recognition*** – Receiving recognition for one's achievements
6. ***Emotional Well Being*** – Solving emotional problems and maintaining self-esteem
7. ***Spiritual Well Being*** – Living according to my spiritual beliefs
8. ***Physical Well Being*** – Taking care of my body
9. ***Sexual Fulfillment*** – Feeling good about myself sexually
10. ***Success and Achievement*** – Meeting one's goals and doing things to one's standards
11. ***Pleasure/Joy*** – Enjoy specific events and situations which heighten pleasure and joy
12. ***Honesty*** – Being straightforward and open
13. ***Cleanliness*** – A clean, fresh appearance of self, home and family members
14. ***Dependability*** – Being able to count on others
15. ***Being known and understood*** – Feeling that my spouse understands me and I understand my spouse
16. ***Extended Family*** – Maintaining relationships with parents and siblings
17. ***Tradition*** – Maintaining family traditions and backgrounds of one's heritage
18. ***Parenthood*** – Having and taking care of children
19. ***Aesthetics*** – Having beauty in my surroundings
20. ***Acceptance*** – Being accepted by people who are important to me
21. ***Sports and Hobbies*** – Having recreational activities I enjoy
22. ***Television and Entertainment*** – Being able to unwind and relax by watching TV and going to movies as well as other entertainment

Family Backgrounds, Values and Expectations

Handout

Are there family of origin issues which really should be explored with professional premarital counselling? The answer is yes, and here is a list of what are considered to be significant family of origin issues:

1. Parental alcoholism – even if the drinking has ceased at the present time
2. Sexual abuse in childhood and adolescence
3. Physical/verbal abuse by either parent directed to any family member
4. Psychiatric illness of any family member
5. Severe communication problems with parents that have resulted in leaving home during adolescence
6. One or both families of origin are not supportive of your engagement and marriage
7. If there is something about your fiancee and his/her relationship with their parents that makes you worried, afraid or disturbed in some way

Being open about these matters now and finding help, if necessary, is the best preventative medicine you can have to make your relationship work in the future.

Good Communication and Nurturing your Relationship

Exercise #1

Sit opposite your partner and take turns completing the following sentences. Remember to maintain eye contact, listen without interrupting, and ask for clarification if you do not understand.

1. When I first met you I thought ______________________________
2. One thing I really like about you is ______________________________

   ____
3. One way in which we are similar is ______________________________
4. One way in which we differ is ______________________________
5. I feel terrific when you ______________________________
6. I get upset when you ______________________________
7. At this moment I feel ______________________________
8. When you get upset I feel ______________________________
9. When you are angry I ______________________________
10. I am afraid to usually talk about ______________________________
11. I wish you would let me ______________________________
12. When I don't want to answer you I ______________________________
13. What I want most from this relationship is ______________________________
14. I hope that we can ______________________________

Good Communication and Nurturing Your Relationship

Exercise #2

Communication Skills Checklist

Rate your communication skills on the following scales by circling the number which best describes yourself. When you are finished, talk with your partner about your experience of doing the checklist and describe those skills you feel you need to work on right now.

1. **Attending**

   When we talk together, I focus my attention on you and what your are saying. I try to take the time needed to really listen.

Rarely		Sometimes		Often
1	2	3	4	5

2. **Clear Intentions**

   I am clear about what I want to say and I try to make sure that my message conveys these intentions.

Rarely		Sometimes		Often
1	2	3	4	5

3. **Mixed Messages**

   I am aware of sending mixed messages to you about my feelings, wants or needs.

Rarely		Sometimes		Often
1	2	3	4	5

4. **Directing**

   I try to let you know in a straightforward way what are my thoughts, feelings, desires or needs about issues, even if it may cause a conflict.

Rarely		Sometimes		Often
1	2	3	4	5

5. **Listening**

   I listen carefully, trying not to interrupt you, jump to conclusions, mind read or construct a response before you have finished speaking.

Rarely		Sometimes		Often
1	2	3	4	5

6. **Clarifying**

After listening, I ask for clarification before responding to your message.

Rarely		Sometimes		Often
1	2	3	4	5

7. **Naming Feelings**

I am able to name my feelings while I am experiencing them.

Rarely		Sometimes		Often
1	2	3	4	5

8. **Taking Responsibility**

I take responsibility for my feelings. I do not blame others for my feelings, but recognize that they are my response to life as I experience it.

Rarely		Sometimes		Often
1	2	3	4	5

9. **"I" Messages**

I try to use "I" messages to express how I feel, what I expect and what I need.

Rarely		Sometimes		Often
1	2	3	4	5

10. **Checking Out Things**

I try to check out what I am hearing and understanding in a conversation to make sure that what I received as a message is what the sender intended.

Rarely		Sometimes		Often
1	2	3	4	5

11. **Keeping on Track**

I try to keep to one issue at a time and stay on track with the issue during the conversation with you.

Rarely		Sometimes		Often
1	2	3	4	5

12. **Positive Regard**

I respect you as a person and try to convey this to you. I try to demonstrate my appreciation for your uniqueness of ideas, feelings and experiences, even when I do not agree or share similar ideas, feelings or experiences.

Rarely		Sometimes		Often
1	2	3	4	5

13. **Self-Disclosure**

I openly express my thoughts and feelings about various issues. I tell you my dreams, desires and needs. I can discuss my strengths and weaknesses without becoming defensive. I let you know what is happening in my private world.

Rarely		Sometimes		Often
1	2	3	4	5

14. **Immediacy**

I let you know on a day-to-day basis what I think and feel about our relationship and communication. I tell you what I like and don't like while it happens.

Rarely		Sometimes		Often
1	2	3	4	5

15. **Informing**

I make specific efforts to give you clear, basic information about things so you can make your plans and decisions.

Rarely		Sometimes		Often
1	2	3	4	5

16. **Sharing**

I take time to share about my private world with you. I do not let situations, reactions, activities and interests interfere in taking time to share.

Rarely		Sometimes		Often
1	2	3	4	5

17. **Affirming**

I make specific efforts to give you positive feedback about your attributes, talents and skills. I tell you how much I appreciate your efforts and I try to give you emotional support.

Rarely		Sometimes		Often
1	2	3	4	5

18. **Confronting**

I take the initiative to bring into the open issues, behaviours and misunderstandings which I feel are hurtful or disappointing to me. I am able to confront you without attacking you and putting you down. I speak about your behaviour and not about your personality.

Rarely		Sometimes		Often
1	2	3	4	5

19. **Negotiating**

I try to initiate finding solutions or a compromise for our disagreements. I avoid trying to badger, manipulate or defeat you in a debate about our disagreements. I avoid a win/lose attitude about disagreeing with you.

Rarely		Sometimes		Often
1	2	3	4	5

20. **Forgiving**

I ask for and express forgiveness to you for wrongdoing. I do not hold grudges or make lists of hurts and failures. I try to cancel any debt of hurt or failure and start over again together as equals.

Rarely		Sometimes		Often
1	2	3	4	5

Good Communication and Nurturing Your Relationship

Exercise #3

Together, review your ratings of each other's Communication Skills Checklist and identify areas of significant differences. Try to explore ways of working together to reduce possible problems from these areas of difference.

Good Communication and Nurturing Your Relationship

Handout

What common communication blocks can work to the detriment of effective communication?

Communication blocks prevent, rather than facilitate, effective communication – particularly when the discussion involves a strongly felt personal issue or concern. These are ways of responding that leave a person feeling bad and less willing to communicate. The person may feel that she or he has not been listened to, not been heard, not been understood. Such blocks produce feelings that the interaction was useless. Here is a list of some of the more common blocks to effective communication, along with some of their possible consequences.

Ordering – This, of course, involves telling the other person what to do. It is often prefaced with "You must . . . " or "You have to . . . " It causes trouble, because it makes the other person feel subordinate and may lead to feelings of resentment and resistance, even if he or she complies. Any acquiescence will increase the person's dependence on authority, thereby undermining his or her self-esteem rather than increasing his or her autonomy.

Advising – This involves offering solutions to personal problems. It is similar to ordering, though it is of a lesser degree. It may be prefaced with such phrases as, "What I would do is . . . " There may be occasions when advice is appropriate (i.e., when it is specifically requested); however, it is often best to let the individual who is wrestling with the personal problem come up with the solutions. The implication in giving advice is that a person cannot solve his or her problems and needs to rely on someone else.

Reassuring – This involves attempting to reassure someone wrestling with a problem that everything is or will be fine, even if it may clearly not be so. Such statements as, "It's O.K . . . " or "Don't worry . . . " characterize this block. The problem with doing this is that it implies a non-acceptance of the speaker's present emotional state of sadness, anger, or whatever. The message is "It's not O.K. for you to feel what you are feeling." That person may feel misunderstood and perhaps even placated and patronized.

Excessive Questioning – This can be a way of distracting someone away from the problem and the feelings associated with it. Questions need to be asked in a way that will be maximally effective; otherwise they can act as a block.

Arguing – This is characterized by phrases such as, "Yes, but . . . " or "You're wrong because . . . " This kind of statement often requires the listener to become defensive and to rally with a counter-argument. Such arguments can result in feelings of inadequacy, inferiority, hostility or a refusal to listen.

Moralizing – This appeal to duty is usually prefaced by phrases such as, "You should . . . or "You ought to . . . " The problem with this kind of statement is that it can produce feelings of guilt and obligations, particularly if there is no desire to do what is being asked.

Criticizing – This involves saying things such as, "You're naive to believe . . . " or "You weren't paying attention." It can have a negative effect on self-esteem. The listener may internally accept the negative judgement and censor further communication to avoid being reprimanded or criticized.

Giving Excessive Praise or Constant Agreement – This block is characterized by statements such as "You were just so wonderful" or "You're right, she really was horrible to you." There are occasions where genuine honest and sincere praise are appropriate, and this comes under the heading of positive feedback. The problems with excessive praise is that it can be seen as manipulative and insincere. It can also generate anxiety if it creates an expectation to meet in the future. Constant agreement can be a way to avoid deeper examination of an issue, problem, or feeling, and it can be a way of closing down, rather than opening up, communication.

Diagnosing – The block is characterized by statements such as, "You're just upset" or "Your problem is . . ." This approach can cause the listener to feel ignored, misunderstood, frustrated, threatened, judged, etc. As a result, he or she may close down communication.

Diverting or Withdrawing – Diverting is a way of turning the conversation away from the issue at hand. It may be recognized by a change of subject or the introduction of some distraction. Withdrawal is characterized by turning away (not attending), having a vacant gaze, or allowing your attention to be distracted. Both of these blocks signal a non-acceptance of what a person is communicating to that person. They imply that the problems are insignificant and that negative emotions are to be avoided or ignored rather than confronted and worked through.

Share *Marriage & Relationships* with a friend

Order ***Marriage & Relationships*** at $12.95 per book plus $3.50 (total order) for postage and handling.

Number of books ______________________x $12.95 = $________
Postage and handling______________________= $ ____3.50
Subtotal ______________________= $ ________
In Canada add 7% GST______________________(Subtotal x .07) = $ ________
Total enclosed ______________________= $ ________

U.S. and international orders payable in U.S. funds./ Price is subject to change.

NAME ______________________

STREET ______________________

CITY______________ PROV./STATE ______________

COUNTRY ______________ POSTAL CODE/ZIP ______________

Please make cheque or money order payable to:

Catholic Family Service Society
Marriage Preparation Program
449 Broad Street North
Regina, Saskatchewan
Canada S4R 2X8

For volume purchases, contact Catholic Family Service Society for volume rates.
Please allow 3-4 weeks for delivery.

Share *Marriage & Relationships* with a friend

Order ***Marriage & Relationships*** at $12.95 per book plus $3.50 (total order) for postage and handling.

Number of books ______________________x $12.95 = $________
Postage and handling______________________= $ ____3.50
Subtotal ______________________= $ ________
In Canada add 7% GST______________________(Subtotal x .07) = $ ________
Total enclosed ______________________= $ ________

U.S. and international orders payable in U.S. funds./ Price is subject to change.

NAME ______________________

STREET ______________________

CITY______________ PROV./STATE ______________

COUNTRY ______________ POSTAL CODE/ZIP ______________

Please make cheque or money order payable to:

Catholic Family Service Society
Marriage Preparation Program
449 Broad Street North
Regina, Saskatchewan
Canada S4R 2X8

For volume purchases, contact Catholic Family Service Society for volume rates.
Please allow 3-4 weeks for delivery.